The World of Herbs & Spices

Created and designed
by the editorial staff
of ORTHO Books

Written by
James K. McNair

Designed by
Linda Hinrichs

Major photography by
Tom Tracy

Herban Renewal

Today we have easy access to herbs and spices gathered from all over the globe. Nostalgic uses, plus appreciation of nature and good foods have led to a renaissance of interest.

A walk through a garden planted with herbs is like a world tour. Plants we use as herbs and spices have been gathered from the temperate and tropical zones of both hemispheres. Many of our favorite seasonings and fragrances from the arid Mediterranean region grow alongside natives from North America and the tropical islands.

When you survey the spice shelves, you're looking at exotic products from all corners of the globe. Many flavorings and fragrances we now take for granted were once costly treasures or just not available at any price. Throughout the centuries herbs and spices have had their ups and downs, periods of great demand followed by dwindling interest. The New World was discovered by Europeans searching for new trade routes to the spice producing areas of Asia. Native American herbs and spices were among the first New World treasures. But by the early years of this century, most Americans were unfamiliar with herbs other than the ubiquitous parsley, mint and a few other basics. Recently, however, there's been a tremendous escalation in the popularity, production and distribution of herbs and spices as garden seed, plants and dried products.

The world of herbs and spices offers an array of exotic imports and home garden harvests, both fresh and preserved for countless uses.

Right: The author grows herbs in suspended gardens and pots in his San Francisco patio.

Nurserymen report a doubling of sales and the retail sales of preserved forms have also doubled in this decade. What lies behind this current revival of interest in herbs and spices?

At the forefront is the new interest in good foods. Americans are looking at foods through more creative eyes. We're fascinated, almost obsessed, with ethnic foods. As the demand for international flavorings has increased, so has the variety of seasonings available at the supermarket or from mail-order suppliers. More people than ever are taking cooking lessons, buying cookbooks and discovering the secrets of great cuisines that rely on herbs and spices. Along the way we've also learned to use seasonings to raise the status of simple dishes and impart new flavors to convenience foods.

The back-to-nature or health movement has also called our attention to herbs and spices. No longer does the phrase "health foods" mean a diet of yogurt and sprouts. Many ethnic influences, greater supplies of fresh produce and creative uses of seasonings as indispensible ingredients have led to a new cuisine that's receiving growing respect.

The popularity of herbs has also grown with the upsurge of interest in gardening. More and more people are discovering the pleasures and economy of homegrown produce. After starting with a few basic herbs, they are soon eager to try others. Nurserymen meet the interest with more of the old species and with new varieties.

Recent years have seen increasing nostalgia for the romance of the past. As a result there's been a great renaissance of crafts. Things are not only made at home for fun but highly skilled craftspeople also are using herbs and spices in papers, candles, dyes for natural fibers and in numerous other almost forgotten arts.

We've rediscovered the simple, sensual pleasures of potpourris and other scents reminiscent of of the Elizabethan garden. Incenses entered the mainstream of our culture in the 1960s during the days of the "flower children." Now many people are planting or purchasing herbs and spices to create fragrances and natural cosmetics.

Other people are ecologists or conservationists in their gardens. Many herbs and spices flourish in a range of climates, require little maintenance, use water sparingly and have built-in pest resistance.

Defining the Terms

Herbs and spices are human experiences rather than scientific categories.

Chefs, perfumers, chemists and horticulturists can give you helpful information but in the end, no certified expert can tell you more about the varied natural substances, collectively labeled herbs and spices than you discover through your own senses.

Botanically speaking, the word "herb" is derived from the Latin *herba,* which means grass or green crops. Most herbs are herbaceous plants, that is, plants whose stems are soft and succulent rather than woody; such plants die entirely or down to the root after flowering. In ordinary language, *the word herb refers to any of that host of plants, both herbaceous and woody, whose leaves, flowers, seeds, roots, bark or other parts we use for flavor, fragrance, medicines, cosmetics or dyes.* Thus, herbs are very general and comprehensive categories of plant life, including many weeds, grasses and hardy vegetables, along with flowers, shrubs and trees.

A question often arises about the pronunciation of the word herb. The oldest form is "erb." It was spelled that way until late in the 15th century when the English added the h, although the h remained silent until the 19th century. Then the h began to be pronounced by people who didn't want to sound Cockney. It still is *h*erb in England, Canada and New

European markets display herb seedlings and mature harvests.

Fields of flowering yellow mustard are scattered from Dijon, France to the California coast.

Medieval herbalist from
a 12th century manuscript.

England. Either way is correct.

The word "spice" comes from the Latin *species,* which means ally. Spices may be thought of as the allies or complements of other substances. They're really defined by how we use them and how they stimulate our senses. *A spice may be any strongly flavored or aromatic substance, obtained from seed, root, fruit, flower or bark that is used in the same ways as herbs.*

Often entire plants are regarded as herbs while only the useful parts or derivatives of plants are true spices. The climbing orchid *Vanilla planifolia,* for example, is not itself a spice. Only its long, pod-like fruit, fermented, cured and marketed as a vanilla bean, and the extract prepared by macerating the bean in an alcohol solution, are spices. On the other hand, the entire sprig of parsley, leaves and stem, is the herb parsley. In fact, the stems of many herbs are richer in the essential oils than their leaves.

To complicate the word difference, the plant commonly called coriander produces green leaves and stems that when eaten fresh or dried are referred to as the herb cilantro or Chinese parsley. When the plant goes to seed, the seeds are usually lumped into the spice category as coriander.

The two terms came into common usage when the early European herbalists referred to useful or delightful plants grown locally as herbs. Those that grew in tropical regions and were transported, for example, by camel along the ancient Cinnamon Route and then via ship, were called spices. The local herbs were ready to use in fresh form, although they were also dried or preserved by other means. But in those days spices could be transported only in dry form to reduce bulk.

To this day we continue to think of herbs as temperate-zone plants that may be used fresh or dried and usually in whole leaf form, while spices are from the East and the tropics, and are dried whole or cut and powdered. But in reality, traditional spices such as ginger root are now grown in temperate climates, even in home gardens.

The real importance of herbs and spices is not what distinguishes them from one another but rather what unites them for us: the pleasures they give us and their usefulness in cooking and other ways.

When you think of spices and herbs as the complements of other substances, you get a notion of proportions. A quart of rice pudding is flavored with a few drops of vanilla or a grating of nutmeg. The single bay leaf in a turkey pie is enough. A few drops of lavender oil will scent a bar of soap.

Herbs and spices are useful in very small quantities because of the potency of their essential oils, and so they appeal to the gardener with limited space and the cook on a budget. But it is good to keep in mind the fact that an herb or spice can be the main event instead of a mere garnish or flourish.

Persian cooks, for example, flavor parsley with lamb; crystallized ginger root is well known in the Orient as a confection; and the Italian pesto, made of freshly ground basil leaves, is used with pasta exactly as a meat sauce is.

Another important fact is that herbs and spices are not inessentials or luxuries. Green herbs are in some cases as rich in nutrients as their vegetable relatives. In the days before invention of refrigerators, freezers and safe canning methods, the spices that preserved foods literally maintained life.

Chinese herbalists today offer the same products that have been historically important through the centuries.

Herbal Roots

Geological excavations and early historical documents show that herbs were important to the ancient Egyptians and Greeks. But there is little doubt that herbs were in regular cultivation in the Orient centuries before they were cultivated and appreciated in the West. According to legend, Chinese medicine was founded by Shen Nung, an herbalist and expert in the creation and use of poisons who lived 2700 years before the birth of Christ.

Like the Occidentals, the Chinese populace had little access to scholarship. In their minds the herbalist was a feared doctor of arcane power, a man in privileged relationship with strange divinities. If in the popular mind the herbalist was a wizard, in the history of horticulture he was a cultivator and cataloger of plants and their properties.

The ancient Chinese custom of perfuming the mouth with cloves before speaking to the emperor required an expert who could provide an aromatic plant at all times of the year. The ability of ginger to preserve meats demanded an herbalist with a keen knowledge about plants and health.

India was for centuries the center of the herb and spice trade. Turmeric, cardamom and cloves have been cultivated in the Indus Valley since 1000 B.C. Many trade routes to India lace the old maps.

The traders brought tales that excited greedy Rome and profits from the spice trade soared. When the Goths overran the western Roman Empire in the 5th century, among the tributes were 3000 pounds of Indian pepper.

Constantine's eastern empire continued trade with India until the Arab conquest cut off European trade with the Far East. From the 7th to the 15th centuries the Arab caliphs monopolized the spice markets, and Europe struggled through into the Dark Ages.

The myths and deliberately frightening fictions of the ancient herbalists descended again on continental Europe. Fortunately during this bleak period herbs and spices were grown and studied in Benedictine and other monasteries.

With the Renaissance the search for trade routes to India was renewed. Columbus was an important figure in the history of herbs and spices. Returning to Spain from the New World he carried loads of allspice, red pepper and cocoa. Together with the native European plants and those brought back from the true Indies, these became the basis of the great Renaissance gardens. Many kinds of herbs for numerous uses were planted together in elaborate formal patterns. In the 1500s the University of Padua could show an herb garden that successfully maintained plants from the Far East, the New World and Europe.

Gathering of sage from a 15th Century miniature.

European settlers brought an array of herbs from their homelands to the Americas. The English planted mint, thyme and angelica. The Germans, Scots and Irish who came to Pennsylvania with William Penn planted their favorites: dill, savory and calendulas. Adapting their plants to new climates and soil conditions, the colonists also domesticated such wild native herbs as goldenrod, sassafras and bayberry. Later immigrants brought herbs from other continents and there were coincidences that would not have happened on any other soil. Cilantro, or coriander, a culinary herb common to Mexico and China, provides an example. Though revered by the Aztecs and rural Mexicans for generations, it was almost entirely unknown in the United States until Chinese laborers on the railroads planted seeds from their homeland near their workcamps. Now coriander is used by Americans of all ethnic backgrounds.

Since the latter half of the 18th century the cultivation of herbs and spices has been the subject of much study and research, with great advances. Test gardens have hybridized new varieties that have achieved culinary and ornamental excellence. And many individuals are now contributing to the science and arts of growing and using herbs and spices.

We want you to meet a few on the next two pages.

Herbalists
of the Present

Betty Rollins is a director of the Herb Society of America. Her garden in Berkeley, California features one of the largest collections of herbs in the West. She gathers rare plants from all over the world and propagates many herbs shared with her by Herb Society friends. Her plants are neatly laid out in an almost scientific manner. Although she uses some in cooking, her main concern is "watching how the plants grow and respond. I like to experience as many plants as possible. I propagate a lot of cuttings and pass them around to other herb gardeners so that a natural disaster here would not wipe out a plant that is rare."

In nearby Oakland, her friend *Helen Ganaway* grows herbs in order to collect petals and leaves for creating some of the most delightful fragrances you've ever

Propagating and sharing rare herbs is a major interest of Betty Rollins.

smelled. A visit with Mrs. Ganaway is a treat to the senses. In the garden there's jasmine, apple mint, old roses, lavender, rosemary and other plants with heady aromas. The house is filled with the faint fragrance of frankincense melting on a low burner. Old apothecary jars containing every imaginable herb and spice line her long hallway. Gallon jugs of dried leaves and petals are stored in a nearby cupboard. "Herbs are nice to use

Helen Ganaway harvests herbs to use in creating special fragrances.

for seasonings and teas," she explains, "but I love them for their fragrance. I've studied all the books on perfumes and scents and hope to write my own version someday. Fragrances bring back so many memories and just lead you on into infinity. Potpourri represents all the summer labors of nature and the herbalist. Mixing day in the fall is a wonderful experience. I blend garden flowers and leaves that have been dried with fixatives and spices from every corner of the globe. You have no idea what a delight until you've tried it."

In the foothills of the San Gabriel Mountains in Southern California *William* and *Norma Jean Lathrop* have designed and planted a garden on the back of a hill, formerly a steep, rocky and weedy area. "Landscaping and maintaining the sloping hillside is a challenge for us. Herbs grow well here due to the natural drainage of the soil, but terracing, regular feeding and lots of water are necessary, too.

"Our interest in herbs was a natural growth of living in this rural area. In discovering the uses of herbs, we've learned more about their importance. Growing and maintaining the plants has become an absorbing hobby. Raised beds of vegetables and herbs are planted in our kitchen garden and over 200 varieties of aromatic, medicinal and culinary plants cover the hillside."

Prolific garden writer, editor and

television personality, *Elvin McDonald* grows herbs under fluorescent lights among a huge collection of *gesneria* and tropical foliage plants in his Manhattan apartment. "Basil is my favorite because it grows so easily along with houseplants in warm temperatures, whereas a lot of the others must have a period of freezing in the fall or else they don't behave too well.

"The other night just as my dinner guests arrived I realized that there was no basil or oregano in the kitchen. One taste of the tomato sauce I was making convinced me that I would have to excuse myself or ask one of my guests to go shopping for herbs. Then I remembered the basil plant that had been growing in one of my bedroom fluorescent light gardens. Earlier in the year all but one pale stem with four leaves had been sacrificed for the treat of fresh pesto sauce for pasta in the middle of a miserable winter. For the first few weeks the lone surviving stem looked like it might expire, but I continued to keep the soil moist, to mist the leaves well and to make light applications of fertilizer.

"After two months of coddling, my weakling had turned into a strong, leafy plant hardly recognizable from its former self. This time I assured it that only a few leaves were needed and this would not be a brutal attack. As I pinched them off, their pungent aroma told me that no trip to the store would

William and Norma Jean Lathrop worked together to design a terraced garden.

be necessary. In fact the leaves that I held in my hand promised better flavor than the dried bottled product could ever impart. Just-picked herb leaves, same as vine-ripened tomatoes, have that illusive quality of tasting unusually good — for me, the way I remember the produce from my mother's farm garden."

Fresh and dried herbs go into Jeanne Rose's natural cosmetics.

Craig Claiborne, noted cooking authority and writer for *The New York Times* wrote, "I do wish that I had closed circuit television so that I could transmit an image to you of me in my herb 'garden.' It is a pathetic plot of ground measuring about 8 feet by 8 feet; it contains, in addition to tarragon, basil, rosemary and sage, a wild accumulation of grass which actually seems to be overtaking the sweet-smelling good things that I grow to go into my cookery. To tell you the truth, I hate to dig in soil."

San Franciscan *Jeanne Rose* is an herbal consultant, author and business woman with her own line of natural cosmetics. She considers fragrance to be medicinal and promotes aroma therapy. Her affair with herbs began about ten years ago while recuperating from an accident. "Someone gave me a little book on herbs and from there I started studying and making things until I reached a point where I knew more than most of the books I was reading as references. My products were better than the ones I was buying and my business came about as a result of the things I made for myself and friends. Ac-

tually, I'd like to see people in all parts of the country making their own cosmetics using things that are fresh from their area."

Jeanne doesn't consider herself to be a gardener, but an herbalist. "To be an herbalist I have to do some gardening in order to have plants to harvest and dry. My garden is so small that I grow only one of everything, mostly just to use them in my personal cosmetics. Ingredients for my retail cosmetics come from commercial herb growers. I'd rather grow green plants with fine smells than beautiful flowers."

Susan Gilmore, who put together many of the handcrafts described in this book and shown in the photos, gathers herbs from her mother's country garden and supplements them with dried versions from a nearby herbal store.

Jacqueline Heriteau, who's written several herb gardening and cooking books, grows as many herbs as she can squeeze onto a Manhattan rooftop to use in cooking.

In New Hampshire, *Barbara Rodgers* has started a commercial herb farm. She began growing herbs because they were needed in cooking, which is her first love. "I found them unavailable fresh, searched out sources of plants, grew my own and found myself providing them to everyone else.

Using herbs and spices in creative crafts interests Susan Gilmore.

By then I had become so interested in growing and using herbs that the herb farm and business was a logical step. We moved to

Michael Landis experiments with herbs to see what works best.

have better land and more of it."

Michael Landis gardens in the midst of a great vineyard in California's Napa Valley, where he conducts test projects for Ortho Books. Michael does not take anyone's word on gardening, but experiments to see what grows best and why. He and his wife Mary report success with herbs indoors, under lights, in greenhouses, hanging baskets and combined with flowers and vegetables in raised beds.

Herb Society

If you would enjoy a continual learning experience and fellowship with herb growers from coast to coast, consider membership in *The Herb Society of America.* In addition to the national group, there are units organized in many states.

The Society sponsors a National Herb Garden at the United States Arboretum in Washington, D.C. A reception area overlooks a formal knot garden. There's a garden of historic roses and fragrances. Small specialty gardens contain collections for teaching and study that include American colonial herbs; culinary, medicinal, commercial, tea, dye and fiber herbs; and native American herb and spice gardens.

For further information write:
The Herb Society of America
2 Independence Court
Concord, MA 01742

Utilitarian Landscapes

Combine beauty and practicality by adding herbs and spices to your landscape, even indoors. They can furnish interesting forms, textures, flowers and colors to any garden design.

If you're inclined to think of herbs in terms of weedy garden plants or a few straggly pots on a kitchen windowsill, think again. Herbs and spices that are planted with a good sense of garden design, given proper culture and kept well-groomed can be among the most beautiful plants in the garden.

The fact that they're useful as flavorings, fragrances, cosmetics, teas or dyes as well as being ornamental is a big bonus to the gardener. As if you needed further reasons for adding them to the garden, many herbs resist drought, repel insects and require little care. This practicality combined with attractiveness makes the plants we call herbs valuable assets to any landscape.

Many of the herbs grown today as ornamentals were originally valued for medicinal or some obscure purposes. We've learned to love them for their historical significance or just for their form, leaf texture, coloration, flowers or other visual aspects.

Tradition has dictated that herbs be relegated to a separate herb garden, either following a formal pattern or planted together informally, or grown without much imagination alongside other good things to eat in the vegetable garden.

The English have always had a special way with herb gardens, arranging the practical plants in attractive designs. At Kew Gardens near London this traditional sunken plan fascinates plant and flower lovers of every age.

A California "tea house" is surrounded by fragrant herbs.

Fortunately for gardeners today, herbs are putting in appearances as part of the total landscape. They're right there alongside flowering bulbs, annuals, perennials and shrubs.

Consider some of the ways herbs can be incorporated into the overall garden picture. Low-growing herbs such as parsley, chives, dwarf sages and thymes are often at their best as borders or edging around flowering beds or planted among annuals and perennials in a blooming border.

They're a pretty and practical edging for tall perennial flowers and and are perfect for filling corners and empty spaces between other plantings. Set out a lot of spreading herbs such as chamomile and creeping thyme to form ground covers or fragrant carpeted garden pathways.

Herbs are attractive combined with the alpines, bulbs and succulents usually grown in rock gardens, an excellent idea for hillsides and slopes. Try plantings of rosemary or wooly thyme to cascade

Stacked weathered boxes provide a multilevel stage for a show of potted herbs, candytuft and daffodils in a small area.

grow them in large tubs or terra-cotta strawberry jars. Since you'll see these herbs often, plant the culinary collection as attractively as any part of the garden. Combine the herbs with edible flowers or those that you'll use as table decorations.

A collection of herbs can be grown in small spaces. A few half-buried cement blocks with plantings in the open areas will provide a small harvest. Remove a few bricks from the patio or wide walkway and add herb plants in the holes, or plant creeping herbs between paving stones. If you have only a balcony, deck or narrow gardening area, go vertical with the planting design. Add shelves, a ladder, stairsteps, or stack wooden or wire boxes or crates to display potted herbs in limited space.

A vertical garden of herbs can flourish with a simple homemade box. Build it as tall and wide as you like but shallow from front to back—no more than about 12 inches. The narrow ends should be solid board but the wide sides are made by crisscrossing slats nailed to the box. Drill drain holes in the bottom. Line the entire insides of the box with heavy-duty plastic sheeting and fill with a lightweight growing medium. Then snip holes in the plastic between the slats and insert roots of young plants. As the herbs grow they'll cover the plastic and you will soon have an outdoor living screen or divider. (See Ortho's book, *Gardening In Containers.*)

A wire pole filled with sphagnum moss and growing medium can be planted just like the hanging basket on page 25. If you make one side flat it can be hung or pushed against a wall to conserve gardening space.

gracefully over terraces of stone, wood or railroad ties.

Anywhere you want a brilliant spot of color add flowering herbs, purple leaf basil or tricolor sage. Subdue an area with one of the grey foliages such as dittany of Crete or gray santolina. Tuck the plants alongside whatever else is growing there, as long as the culture is compatible.

For a shaded woodsy area, plant fernlike chervil or sweet cicely. Sweet woodruff, mints and violets are good company for these shade-tolerant plants as ground cover under trees.

Unusual herb gardens can be designed with plants that grow in water. Add papyrus, water chestnut, lotus or other plants to a shallow pool or large tub for a cooling spot of water. Another subject too long for this book is hydroponic gardening. Many herbs can be adapted to this specialized form of growing in water with regular additions of nutrients. Most local garden centers offer hydroponic units and supplies.

Herbs do not have to be confined to a permanent place in the garden. Container-grown plants can be moved about as needed to fill in empty spots or to stage instant garden shows on a patio, deck or terrace. Container choice is part of the landscape design to

achieve the look you want. See page 24 for ideas.

Suspend plants in baskets or hanging pots from roof overhangs, tree branches or posts with arms. Flat-sided wire baskets of herbs and spices can hang on fences, walls or any similar surface. Plant trailing rosemary and thymes to spill out of window boxes. Combine them with upright herbs and vegetables.

Plant variations on themes with a basket of spaghetti sauce herbs, collections of one type of plant with several varieties, such as thyme, a tub of assorted mints for teas, planters of your favorite *bouquet garni* herbs, or a mixture of lettuce and other salad greens with herbs that will end up in the same bowl.

The adventuresome gardener can try a hand at special shapes. Dig old plants with woody stems such as oregano and rosemary from the garden, put them in pots, trim and train to grow as a bonsai. Remove the side shoots along a single woody upright stem and shape the foliage at the top as a tree or standard. Prune and train boxwood, myrtle or any compact woody herb into geometric or whimsical topiary shapes.

No doubt you'll want to keep a few culinary herbs near the kitchen door. If there's no garden space,

At the Huntington Library Gardens in San Marino, California we found a colorful display of herbs that were grown in Elizabethan gardens. A free-flowing band of calendulas or pot marigolds is edged with purple violas and clumps of germander. The bird bath adds a focal point to the design. Beyond are old roses and other sweet-smelling plants that were treasured in traditional herb gardens. Home gardeners would probably not devote this amount of space to one kind of flowering herb, but the design idea can be modified to fit the available space.

Designing the Outdoor Garden

Should you wish to follow tradition and have a special garden devoted to herbs there are two ways to go: formal or informal designs.

Formal herb gardens came about during the Middle Ages and are characterized by symmetrical design, often with geometric planting patterns. These planting areas or *parterres* are traditionally bounded with a manicured low edging of boxwood, santolina or other compact herb that can be kept shaped and controlled. Bricks, large stones or strips of weathered wood can also be used as edging.

The formal garden usually features paths of brick, stone, crushed stone or gravel running in geometrical patterns among the beds. Alternative materials for paths include shells or hulls and other organic material indigenous to your area. The focal point of the garden can be a spectacularly tall specimen plant, a birdbath, fountain, bee skep of twisted straw or sundial or other garden sculpture.

Planted or empty urns are often placed symmetrically in the garden.

The Elizabethan formal garden was characterized by the famous interwoven knot or ribbon planting. You can choose to duplicate a design steeped in history or create your own version. Work out the planting idea on paper, then transfer it to the garden by setting out wooden stakes and marking off the planting area with stretched string. Use a middle stake with a string to form circles and curves. Choose plant material that can be easily shaped to definite form and will stay compact when clipped. Sage, bush basil, lemon thyme, spearmint, peppermint, santolina and boxwood are good candidates. The open areas remaining can be mulched over with crushed stones or organic matter to set off the knot and keep weeds away.

The informal herb garden is free-form with plants irregularly spaced to look natural. Informal designs are typified by the picturesque cottage garden of towering hollyhocks and delphiniums over great clumps of lavenders interplanted with all sorts of foliage and flowers. But there are many other ways to develop informal designs including rock gardens, terraces, raised beds, woodland scenes and contemporary modular sections devoted to each herb.

Whereas the formal garden utilizes herbs and spices that can be kept under control, the informal garden design relies heavily on rambling herbs such as mints, catnip, lemon balm, scented geraniums and shrub roses. Informal gardens can also use a few garden accessories casually placed.

No matter what your choice of design remember to include places to sit among the plants and enjoy their fragrances and beauty. Maybe it's simply a railing or cap on the edge of a raised bed, a weathered wooden bench or well-designed traditional or modern garden furniture. Choose whatever fits the design and mood of your landscape.

Whether you choose a formal or wilder version of the herb garden, go about the planning in the same way. Begin with a study of garden catalogs and books. Visit public and private gardens to see what you'd like to grow. Perhaps you want only culinary plants or just those with memorable fragrances. Many people choose to follow a theme and plant all the herbs mentioned in the Bible or in the writings of Shakespeare, or the herbs that were common to a particular historical period. Other popular themes include native American herbs, lemon-scented foliages, gardens that attract bees, an herbal tea garden, or only flowering plants. We describe such gardens later. Your creative mind can add numerous themes and variations.

Give your attention first to the overall form and shapes you want in your garden. Make a list of plants that can fulfill the total landscape design, starting with those you really want to grow and adding others that are necessary to satisfy the design.

Then turn your thoughts to coloring the design. Choose varie-

Colorful tin food cans seem right at home as containers for a group of herbs growing on a sunny kitchen windowsill. Fresh herbs are handy for the cook.

ties of the plants on your list that bloom or have foliages in the right hues. Create a riot of color, go all white and green or keep the flower or leaf color monochromatic. One of the prettiest herb gardens combines only gray foliages.

Once you have your plant list, check each plant's requirements for light and cultural care to see how many you can provide with the right amount of sunlight and proper soil. Divide the plants into groups according to their requirements and plan to group those with like needs together. However, herbs are so versatile that the groupings don't have to be strict.

It's important to keep growth habits such as height and spread in mind when you determine what to plant where. Common sense tells us to plant tall herbs as hedges, backgrounds or accents and to vary the heights so everything has a chance to receive the sun and be seen. Make a diagram of your garden space on paper and position new beds, plants, paths and accessories in combination with the existing trees and large shrubs that you want to retain. Then take the diagram to the garden and walk through your idea, making any necessary changes. Now you're set to do the planting yourself or turn to a garden contractor.

Whenever you plant an herb, especially an unusual one, you'll want to add labels. There are wooden, metal and plastic markers available from nursery suppliers. If you don't find something you can live with, design your own of wood, slate or other material to blend into the garden. Some gardeners use wooden cooking spoons, for example, in their culinary herbs.

When you establish a new garden, try to be patient — it takes several years to get a full, lush garden going.

Any garden, especially herbs that tend to go straggly if unattended, will not retain their original good looks without regular grooming and maintenance.

If you'll have to do all the gardening yourself, keep the landscape design simple and build in easy maintenance. If you're new to gardening, start with only a few common, easy-to-grow herbs that appeal to you. Many are described on pages 36–47. Learning to grow these well before moving on to others saves disappointment and builds gardening confidence. As you learn, don't be afraid to experiment with new plants, new ways to grow the tried and true or innovations in garden design.

Designing the Indoor Garden

If your landscape is limited to the indoors, foremost consideration must be given to meeting the cultural requirements. You can't just put plants where they'll look pretty or where you'd like a bit of greenery. A check of available sunlight usually defines the space you have for herb gardening, unless you add sufficient artificial lighting to meet the high footcandle requirements of most herbs and spices.

For a successful interior landscape choose containers in colors and materials that fit the interior design of the room they'll go in. Classic clay goes with everything. See page 24 for other ideas.

Group the indoors plants just as you would arrange an outdoor flower bed, with tall plants as backgrounds for low-growing species or as accents among a grouping of lower plants. Blend herbs with more traditional tropical house plants and flowering species. Utilize trailing herbs to soften the hard-edged look of shelves, tabletops or windowsills. Group hanging herbs in the sun on different levels to create a visually pleasing design of suspended forms. Choose hanging hardware with attention to the design and what looks best in the room.

The key to making the most of herbs and spices, whether indoors or in the outdoor garden, is a new appreciation of the plant itself. Look at it for its visual contributions to the garden as well as the many ways to use the harvest of flowers, leaves, stems, seeds and roots. Keep the plants looking great by learning all you can about how to grow them.

Herb Garden Themes

Of the many ways herbs and spices can be grouped, their uses and pleasures for us come first. The accompanying plant lists describe a few themes for your variations, along with plants for special purposes.

(See index or common name directory on inside back cover.)

Shakespeare Garden

Listed below are nonpoisonous herbs mentioned in the writings of William Shakespeare. All were popular in Elizabethan England.

Bay
Burnet
Calendula
Carnation
Chamomile
Columbine
Dyer's broom
Flax
Hyssop
Johnny-jump-up
Lavender
Lemon balm
Marjoram
Mint
Mustard
Myrtle
Parsley
Pink
Rose
Rosemary
Savory
Strawberry
Thyme
Wormwood

Good Cook's Garden

Most of the plants on this list are indispensable ingredients in the kitchen. You may want to plant them near the kitchen door to save steps.

Angelica
Anise
Basil
Bay
Borage
Burnet
Caraway
Chervil
Chives
Chrysanthemum, garland
Coriander
Costmary
Cumin
Dill
Garlic
Horehound
Horseradish
Hyssop
Lavender
Leek
Lovage
Marjoram
Mint
Mustard
Nasturtium
Onion
Oregano
Parsley
Peppers, chiles
Rocket
Rose
Rosemary
Sage
Savory
Sesame
Shallot
Sorrell
Tarragon
Watercress

Tea Garden

Almost every herb and spice can be made into a tea. These are especially good and will make an attractive planting as well. If your climate is quite warm, add the oriental tea plant and ginger.

(For making herbal teas, see page 62.)

Angelica
Basil
Bergamot
Borage
Catnip
Chamomile
Costmary
Dill
Fennel
Goldenrod
Hibiscus
Horehound
Jasmine
Lemon balm
Lemon verbena
Lovage
Marjoram
Mint
Parsley
Rose
Rosemary
Sage
Sarsaparilla
Sassafras
Speedwell
Strawberry
Sweet cicely
Sweet woodruff
Tansy
Thyme
Wintergreen
Wood betony

Garden of Fragrances

A walk through a garden designed for fragrances is a delight to all the senses. Not only do they smell great but they're visually pleasing, taste good and you can't resist touching the leaves as you listen to the birds and bees enjoying them, too.

Angelica
Basil
Bayberry
Bergamot
Burnet
Catnip
Chamomile
Costmary
Gas plant
Good-King-Henry
Heliotrope
Hyssop
Jasmine
Lavender
Lemon balm
Lemon verbena
Lily-of-the-valley
Marjoram
Mint
Oregano
Pennyroyal
Rose
Rosemary
Sage
Savory
Scented geraniums
Southernwood
Sweet cicely
Sweet flag
Sweet olive
Sweet woodruff
Tansy
Tarragon
Thyme
Valerian
Violet
Yarrow

A bust of the writer overlooks the Shakespeare Garden at Huntington Library.

Dyer's Garden

Among the many plants used as natural dyes are these that make attractive additions to the landscape.

Agrimony
Ajuga
Birch
Blackberry
Bloodroot
Coltsfoot
Cornflower
Dandelion
Elder
Elecampane
Goldenrod
Hibiscus
Hollyhock
Hyssop
Indigo, wild
Lady's mantle
Larkspur
Lily-of-the-valley
Onion
Parsley
Saffron crocus
Sassafras
Sorrel
Sunflower
Tansy
Violet
Yarrow

The Flowering Garden

A well-planned garden of herbs and spices can provide a lot of flowers for fragrances, cutting, drying, eating, garnishing or just enjoying. Many other herbs flower, but should be harvested just before flowers open.

Angelica
Anise
Bergamot
Borage
Calendula
Carnation
Chrysanthemum
Chamomile
Chervil
Columbine
Coriander
Costmary
Cumin
Dandelion
Delphinium
Dill
Elecampane
Fennel flower
Foxglove
Ginger
Goldenrod
Great mullein
Heliotrope
Hollyhock
Hyssop
Johnny-jump-up
Larkspur
Lavender
Lily-of-the-valley
Lovage
Marsh mallow
Mustard
Narcissus
Pink
Rose
Rosemary
Safflower
Saffron crocus
Sunflower
Sweet woodruff
Tansy
Thyme
Violet
Yarrow

Gray and Silver Garden

A quiet garden of subtle shimmering foliages is a pleasant place to visit, especially on a moonlight evening. Gray foliage highlights the colors of the flowers of these plants and their companions, and provides contrast from vivid flower beds.

Aloe
Apple mint
Carnation
Clary sage
Dwarf sage
Germander
Grey santolina
Horehound
Lamb's ears
Lavender
Nutmeg geranium
Oregano
Pineapple mint
Rosemary
Silver sage
Silver tansy
Silver thyme
Southernwood
Wormwood
Yarrow

Medieval Garden

Among the many plants protected within walled monastery gardens of the Middle Ages are these herbs, still popular centuries later.

Angelica
Caraway
Columbine
Chives
Iris
Johnny-jump-up
Lavender
Lemon balm
Marjoram
Mint
Pennyroyal
Pink
Rose
Rosemary
Sage
Santolina
Shallot
Strawberry
Southernwood

Bee Garden

A garden composed of these plants will be a special delight to gardeners who are beekeepers or those who just enjoy the buzzing around on a summer's day.

Basil
Bergamot
Borage
Catnip
Chamomile
Fennel, sweet
Germander
Hyssop
Lavender
Lemon balm
Marjoram
Oregano
Red clover
Rosemary
Sage
Sweet cicely
Thyme
Winter savory

Indoor Garden

When you plan an indoor herb and spice garden, start with these easy-to-grow plants. If there's insufficient sunlight, group them in an attractive unit under wide-spectrum artificial light.

Aloe
Basil
Bay
Borage
Burnet
Chervil
Chives
Dill
Dittany of Crete
Fennel
Ginger
Hyssop
Lavender
Lemon balm
Lemon verbena
Lovage
Marjoram
Mint
Oregano
Parsley
Pennyroyal
Rosemary
Sage
Savory
Scented geraniums
Sorrel
Sweet olive
Tarragon
Thyme

Herbs serve many
landscape functions
such as groundcovers
and borders.

Herbs for Ground Cover

Ajuga
Bedstraw
Catnip
Chamomile
Creeping thymes
Germander
Lamb's ears
Lily-of-the-valley
Mint
Pennyroyal
Red clover
Rosemary
Santolina
Speedwell
Star jasmine
St. John's wort
Sweet woodruff
Violet
Wintergreen

Herbs for Hedges

Angelica
Bergamot
Costmary
Germander
Hyssop
Lovage
Oregano
Pineapple sage
Rosemary
Sweetbriar rose
Tansy

Herbs for Low Borders and Edging

Boxwood
Chamomile
Chives
Dwarf or bush basil
Dwarf rosemary
Dwarf sage
Hyssop
Parsley
Santolina
Savory
Thyme

Herbs to Repel Insects

Basil
Bay
Bergamot
Borage
Catnip
Chamomile
Chervil
Chives
Dill
Garlic
Horseradish
Lavender
Lemon balm
Lovage
Marjoram
Mint
Oregano
Pennyroyal
Rosemary
Sage
Santolina
Savory
Southernwood
Tansy
Tarragon
Thyme
Wormwood
Yarrow

Getting Down to Basics

Here is everything you need to know to grow herbs and spices successfully. Class them as easy-to-grow outdoors, indoors, in containers, even under lights.

In spite of all the lore surrounding the use of herbs and spices, growing them is no more difficult than growing ordinary flowers and vegetables. In this book we'll point out the *ideal* conditions for *optimum* growth, but keep in mind that you can have success with annual herbs by planting and growing them right along with your other annual vegetables and flowers. Treat the perennial plants just as you would the ornamentals and you'll probably be pleased with their response.

It would be impossible to satisfy the ideal conditions for all the herbs in the small garden space usually devoted to them but you can count on plenty of seasonings if you consider herbs as a group and think of them as part of the vegetable garden. With many herbs such as mint, bee balm and tarragon the problem is keeping them under control once they're in the garden.

Most of the plants classed as herbs are hardy, easy to grow, practically immune to diseases and pests, adaptable to many types of soil and growing conditions, and quite tolerant of drought and neglect. Of course, like any group of plants, they'll reward you well if you pay attention to their simple wants and needs.

William and Norma Jean Lathrop spend many pleasurable hours each week in their herb garden. As they discover more things to grow, the garden continues to expand over a steep hillside by means of terraces and raised beds.

Garden centers all over the world offer headstarts by means of herb transplants.

The Outdoor Garden

Whether you have a few plants growing near the kitchen door, rows of herbs among the vegetables or cutting flowers, or a large formal garden, the techniques of outdoor gardening remain the same in most climates.

Selecting the Best Exposure

Most herbs and spices require full sunlight for at least 5 to 8 hours a day. Quite a few are tolerant of partial shade and some forest natives enjoy the shade. Check the individual plant requirements on pages 36–45.

Preparing the Site and Soil

Most home grown plants described in this book prefer well-drained soil. Exceptions to the rule include horseradish, ginger, sweet flag and woodruff, which all enjoy moist rich soil around their roots. A few plants even grow directly in water. But for the vast majority of herbs and spices an ideal planting site would be a gentle incline with sandy soil.

If your garden doesn't have good natural drainage you have two options: a raised bed and soil amendment.

Raised beds have been a part of herb gardening since ancient times. All you need is something that will hold about 6 inches of

To transplant herbs into the garden, prepare a hole in amended soil.

Tap the plant from it's container and position it in the earth.

After firming the soil (above), water and add the label (below).

soil above the normal ground level. Railroad ties, fence posts, cement blocks or stones can be used as the bed walls, or you can use redwood boards held in place with 2×4s. A wood railing nailed to the top will let you sit while you maintain and harvest the herbs or just enjoy their textures and fragrances.

Once you've built the bed, fill it with fresh soil. If it is a small bed, you can purchase one of the packaged synthetic soils such as Jiffy-Mix or Redi-Earth formulated to provide good drainage and balanced support for the roots.

Planting Mix

For larger beds it's economical and easy to make your own mix:
9 cubic feet fine sand
9 cubic feet peat moss
9 cubic feet ground bark
5 pounds 5-10-10 fertilizer
7 pints ground limestone
1 pound iron sulphate.
These amounts will give you 6 inches of soil in a bed measuring about 6 feet by 6 feet.

If you do not want a raised bed for your herbs, you can improve drainage and soil by excavating the planting area to a depth of about a foot. Separate the topsoil from the subsoil into two piles and break up large clods. Spread 2 to 4 inches of crushed rock or large gravel in the excavation.

Add 1 part sand to 3 parts subsoil, mix well and fill the area a little over half way. Then blend in 1 part organic matter (compost, manure, peat moss, leaf mold or sawdust) to 3 parts topsoil and fill up the planting area.

Use a soil test kit to determine the pH of your soil if you are in doubt or have a sample checked at your nearby agricultural extension service office. The pH is a measure of relative acidity and alkalinity: if the pH is 7 the soil is neutral, below 7 the soil is acidic and above 7 it is alkaline. Most herbs enjoy a range of 6.0 to 7.5 but a few prefer more alkaline soil. If your soil is found to be too acidic, add 5 pounds finely ground limestone to each 100 square feet of planting area in order to raise the pH about a half to a full point. Alkaline soil can be changed the same amount by adding ½ pound ground sulphur or 3 pounds aluminum sulfate or iron sulfate to each 100 square feet.

Planting the Garden

Seed and transplants of common herbs are available at garden centers, nurseries, plant shops or from mail-order suppliers. You'll have to order the more unusual varieties from specialized catalogues (see page 93) or secure them from herb-growing friends.

If you need only a few plants, it's easiest to buy little ones from a local source. They're ready to transplant for an almost instant herb garden.

To remove a plant from a container, follow these simple steps: About 30 minutes before attempting the move, water thoroughly so the root system and soil will hold together well.

Hold the pot with one hand and put the other hand over the top, with the plant stem between two fingers.

Turn the pot upside down and tap the rim against the edge of a table or bench to loosen the rootball.

Then lift the pot away.

Make a hole in the garden soil or bed mix large enough to accommodate the rootball and slip the plant in place with the soil at the same level on the plant as it was in the container. Add a little more soil around the plant and firm with fingers to eliminate air pockets. Water thoroughly and put identification sticks or labels at the base of the plant.

If you want a head start on the season, you can begin seeds indoors in late winter (see page 27). However, most seeds thrive better if sown in the garden as soon as all danger of frost is past and the soil begins to warm up. Some seeds that require a long germination period can be planted in the late fall for the following growing season. Follow the planting times recommended on the seed packets for your local climate.

Herbs look best and grow well when planted in large expanses or clumps rather than neat rows. Rake the freshly prepared bed and scatter the seeds evenly over the area. Cover with soil to the depth recommended on the seed packet—usually twice the seed diameter. Firm the topsoil with your hands or a board and mist the planting area with water.

Always label all seed beds as soon as you've planted them so you'll know what is growing where.

If you want to plant seeds in rows, make shallow furrows in the prepared soil with a rake. Sow seed in the furrows at the distance suggested on the packet. Firm and moisten as above.

If your garden is plagued by birds, cover the planting area with screening until seeds germinate. Keep the soil moist, but never soggy, throughout germination. Normally annuals take about two weeks and perennials about three to four weeks or longer to germinate; check the seed packet.

You can stretch the harvest season of some short-cycle herbs such as coriander and borage by making successive sowings several weeks apart.

When the little plants are up and have formed two pairs of true leaves, thin out overcrowded areas. The thinnings of culinary herbs are delicately flavored and can be used in foods, or you can transplant healthy thinnings to another spot in the garden or to containers.

When the plants are several inches tall, they may benefit from a covering of mulch. Mulches keep weeds under control, set off the herbs visually, retain moisture and keep the soil at a cool and even temperature. Organic materials such as bark chips, chunky peat moss, pine needles and straw, or small gravels, are natural companions to herbs. Plastic sheeting isn't good around herbs because it tends to retain too much surface moisture and doesn't allow enough air circulation.

Watering and Feeding

Frequent light spraying with the garden hose is a poor method of watering because it supplies moisture only to the topsoil. Herbs need deep soaking that penetrates the ground at least 12 inches. Use a handheld hose if you have the patience but a soaker hose is more convenient and effective. Let it run for a couple of hours each time you water, preferably in the morning so the plants will have time to dry off before dark.

Avoid overwatering but at the same time, never allow the soil

to dry out completely. For routine watering some gardeners use the rule of thumb—don't water until you see a few leaves beginning to wilt, then water thoroughly. A more accurate test is to insert your finger into the soil which, if it's beginning to dry out a half-inch below the surface, needs water.

A few herbs and spices require moist soil at all times and some prefer it very dry. Consult the specific requirements on pages 36–45.

Although herbs don't need the large amounts of fertilizer that many other plants do, they respond to moderate feedings once or twice a year. Feed in the spring with a balanced fertilizer such as 5-10-5 and again in late summer to help carry the herbs on through fall. Too much fertilizer makes the soil overly rich and results in lush foliage that has only small amounts of fragrant oils. However, some of the plants mentioned in this book—such as the flowering shrubs—require more and heavier feedings than the normal herbs for optimum growth.

Controlling Pests and Diseases

The fragrant oils in herb leaves that make them attractive to people also repel insects and make the plants resistant to diseases. Occasionally pests such as aphids or red spider mites will attack herbs. Hose them off edible herbs with a strong stream. Nonedibles can be sprayed with malathion to control insects.

Keep an eye out for pests in roses and other flowering shrubs that grow alongside herbs and spray with appropriate chemicals at the first sign of attack, unless you plan to eat the blooms. Then treat organically with the hose or cut away infested parts. Always spray carefully to avoid wind drift onto edible herbs.

Slugs and snails agree with good cooks about the taste of tender young herbs. Should they move in on your garden, immediately sprinkle the area with snail bait, following label directions. For use around culinary herbs, select formulas recommended for vegetables. If these slimy pests are common in your garden, put out the bait when you first plant to protect the seedlings.

Add vermiculite to container soil to insure fast drainage.

Holding the plant securely, tap the roots out of the container.

Position plant in new pot (above), firm the soil and water well (below).

Spaghetti sauce herbs are combined in a flat-sided wire basket.

Containers range from strawberry jars *(above)* to bleached wooden tray *(below)*.

Children can be quite creative when it comes to containers for herbs.

Protecting Herbs in Winter

After the leaves of perennial plants wither in the fall, cut the stalks down to ground level. In cold regions, evergreen perennials should be dug up, potted in containers and moved indoors before frost.

New Englander Barbara Rogers advises, "With a little extra attention to the less hardy varieties, the herb gardener in the North can be just as successful as one in a kinder climate. The annuals are fast growing enough to mature in a short season and most perennials herbs are winter hardy.

"Rosemary, bay, lemon verbena, sweet marjoram and some of the thymes are not hardy and can be brought indoors to winter over and all make attractive houseplants in the process. Lemon verbena will wilt, loose its leaves and appear to be dying. This is just its natural seasonal defoliation. Give it light, but water sparingly and, as spring approaches, it will sprout new leaves."

Some people like to extend the season for fresh herbs by digging annuals that are still productive from the outdoor garden and potting them for growing indoors.

When you move herbs indoors, wash them in soapy water to get rid of aphids and red spiders that may be hiding and could wreak havoc with other houseplants.

In regions where the ground freezes, mulch over the outdoor perennial herb garden after the first freeze. Plants should remain frozen all winter and not be subjected to alternative freezing and thawing. Cover thickly with straw, leaves, marsh or salt hay or evergreen boughs to allow air to get through. Leave the mulch on until all frost danger is past.

Confining the Spread of Herbs

If you want just a small area of tarragon, mint or other herb that spreads rapidly, plant it in a clay pot with soil about an inch below the rim, then sink it into the ground deep enough that the soil levels in the pot and the ground are even.

Instead of pots you can sink a wooden box, header boards or metal strips 6 to 8 inches into the soil.

The Container Garden Indoors/Outdoors

Herbs and spices are good candidates for container gardening. They're easy to grow, adaptable and enjoy the good drainage that pots and other containers allow. Often herbs look more attractive thus displayed than lost or tucked away outdoors. Best of all, potted herbs allow for a lot of versatility in meeting their cultural needs throughout the year. The containers can be shifted all around the garden, deck, patio or from room to room as sun patterns change with the seasons. For gardeners with limited space, growing herbs in containers is an obvious convenience.

In a sunny window, under artificial lighting or with a combination of the two, herbs can keep on growing all winter. Then they can go to the outdoors when the weather warms up or, if their simple growing requirements can be met, remain indoors year-round.

The Container

Although many people prefer the totally natural look of clay pots, any type of container that has good drainage and enough room for the plant's roots can be a winner.

Among the more popular containers for herbs are plastic pots, all one color or mixed according to their setting. A point to remember is that plants in plastic pots need watering only about a third as often as clay containers because the plastic isn't porous.

You can adapt any kind of container to herb growing, so there's no need to stop with traditional pots. Consider clear Lucite in cubes or other geometric shapes, colorful glazed ceramics, wooden planters and tubs and half-barrels, clay strawberry jars, coffee canisters and other kitchen cans. There are flats and wooden trays, racks to hold 4-inch pots—soda pop cartons will do—wire baskets, wicker baskets with metal or plastic liners, and hanging containers in many designs.

Don't forget to put the right type of saucer or tray under containers indoors. Moisture seeping through unglazed clay can damage table-tops and floors, so you're better off with plastic, glass, rubber, china, or other nonporous catchers. A layer of small pebbles in the saucer will keep the container's drainage holes above water.

There are so many great containers from which to choose, there's no excuse for selecting one that has no drainage, no matter how pretty it looks. It makes watering too complicated. Save it for water plants, rooting cuttings, or cut flowers.

The Potting Soil

The easiest and surest way to go is packaged potting mix. It provides good drainage and can be used as is for most plants we describe in this book. If a particular herb requires rich soil (see pages 36–45) just add an equal quantity of organic matter such as leaf mold or peat moss to the packaged mix. If very fast drainage is required, mix an equal part of perlite or sand with the packaged formula.

Potting and Transplanting

Plant one kind of herb per pot or combine several in a container garden. Remember to plant together only those that are compatible in their water, soil and light requirements.

Make sure the container is clean and cover the drainage hole with a piece of broken pottery, curved side up, or a piece of galvanized screening wire to keep soil from washing into and clogging the drainage hole. Put a little potting soil in the bottom.

Remove the plant from its old container as described on page 22 and place the plant in the new container so that it sits comfortably with the top of its rootball about an inch below the rim. Add soil mix around the sides and with your fingers compress the soil all around the roots to eliminate air pockets. Water until the container drains.

Incidentally, it's a good idea to remove plants from their containers about twice a year to see if the rootball has become too tight. If you've noticed that leaves wilt in spite of good cultural habits, it's probably repotting time.

Planting a Mossed Herb Basket

There's something about the look of a mossy basket that seems just right for a mixture of culinary herbs to hang near the kitchen door or wherever there's good sunlight. It's easy to make and rewards you with seasonings for many months.

The materials you need are:
Wire basket, available in many sizes and shapes from garden centers, to hang from above or flat against a wall
Hardware for hanging
Green sphagnum moss to fill basket
Soil mix
Seedlings (about 2 dozen for a 10 inch basket)

Soak the moss in a container of water for about 15 minutes while you attach the hardware and hang the basket at a comfortable level for planting.

Take a piece of moss about 6 inches square and squeeze the water from it. Fold in half with mossy side out and slide in between the top two horizontal wires of the basket by pressing the moss together. When you let go, the natural springiness of the moss will hold it in place.

Push the piece of moss against a vertical wire and align with the top of the basket. Insert another piece of moss in the same way and move it tightly against the first piece. Repeat this procedure until

there's a tight collar of moss around the top of the basket.

With large pieces of moss line the inside and bottom of the basket, overlapping each piece so that soil cannot leak through. After lining, trim away straggly pieces with scissors.

Put about 2 inches of moist soil in the bottom. Poke a hole from the side through the moss so that a plant's rootball can be inserted. Bend the wires if necessary. Remove the little plant from its container and gently shake off loose soil. Insert the roots through the wire frame and moss so the rootball lies on the surface of the soil mix and the crown of the plant just touching the inside of the moss lining. Place more plants in this way until the bottom row is complete.

When the bottom of the basket has been planted, add another inch or so of soil and inset another row of plants around the basket. Continue planting until you reach the moss collar. Then add soil to within one inch of the basket top. Plant the top as you would any other container.

As plants grow you can train them as you wish by positioning the stems with pins or bent pieces of wire stuck into the mossed basket. Feed and water them as you would ordinary container plants and harvest them freely to encourage full growth.

The Right Light and Atmosphere

Although most herbs enjoy full sun, containerized plants lack the insulation around their roots that a garden provides. Pots outdoors should be put in partial shade during the hot part of the summer day.

Check the recommended light for each plant indoors or out and find a spot with that amount of light. During the year as the sun shifts, you'll need to reposition the pot. That's part of the advantage of containerized gardening.

The indoor gardener might give thought to a window greenhouse, especially for culinary herbs. Easy-to-install prefabricated units are available or you can build your own with a simple framework of 2×4s encased in heavy plastic.

If you haven't a place indoors that gets at least 5 hours a day of direct sun, add artificial lighting. Artificial light can also be the sole source, in which case you have to assure that the plants get the full spectrum of light waves they need. It can come from various combinations of fluorescent and incandescent lights or, more easily, from the wide-spectrum fluorescents. These tubes—available in standard fixture lengths—come close to providing all the wavelengths in natural daylight in the proper proportions for plants to thrive.

Fixtures can be mounted underneath shelves, window sills or kitchen cupboards to shine down on counter tops, or hidden inside cabinets. With hood reflectors to bounce light down on the leaves, units can be attached to carts, hung from the ceiling or supported over tabletops.

There are a number of simple plant stands, carts, tabletop units, and 'grow-light' furniture pieces on the market. Just plug them in, add plants and have an herb garden where you never thought possible.

The closet, basement, hallway can flourish with herbs all year long. The designing gardener can install herb and spice light gardens that are as attractive as any outdoor bed or window display.

Lights should operate 14 to 18 hours per day. Install a simple automatic timer that turns the lamps on and off regardless of your memory.

The top of the foliage should never be closer than 5 or 6 inches from the lamp and never more than 15 to 18 inches below. Most prefabricated light units have adjustable mountings to raise and lower the light as plants grow. With unmoveable fixtures, set small plants on inverted pots or saucers, taking away the supports as the plants grow taller.

When gardening with artificial light, follow all the other plant care and maintenance guidelines given below for container-grown herbs.

If you discover the roots are overgrown, loosen them by hand, shake off loose soil and repot in a container that is one size larger. An alternative method is to cut through the root system from top to bottom in two places and across the bottom, and remove about a third of the rootball. Prune away the same amount of foliage growth and repot in a container that is one size larger.

Water and Food

It's time to water if the soil a half inch below the surface is dry. Overwatering is the biggest hazard to plants indoors. Too often they're drowned with kindness. Putting your finger a half inch into the soil is the most reliable way to tell when it's time to water. Apply water until it runs through to the saucer. Let it stand for half an hour, then pour off any excess water from the drainage saucer.

Don't allow the soil to dry out completely or the rootball will shrink and then water will just run down the inside of the pot and escape before the thirsty plant can use it. If a plant has gone so long without water that the soil is hard and dry, submerge the pot under water for several minutes or until air bubbles stop rising from the soil surface. Let it drain for about half an hour.

Outdoor containers should be checked every couple of days. Plants in them usually require watering more often than their counterparts growing in the garden.

Container-grown plants can't reach out for nutrition as their garden relatives do, so they benefit from regular additions of one of the balanced fertilizers formulated for houseplants. Always water the plant before feeding. Fertilize mildly from early spring to fall but use only about half the strength and apply only half as often as recommended on the product label.

Indoor herbs appreciate extra humidity. Pebbles in the drainage tray with a little water in the bottom make the air immediately around the plants more humid. A dish of water set among the plants helps in a similar way. Misting the foliage as you do other houseplants not only adds humidity but helps keep the leaves clean. Every few weeks it's a good idea to immerse the foliage in tepid water to wash away the accumulated dust and household grease.

Herbs indoors enjoy as much fresh air as possible. Keep them near a window that can be opened, provided the temperature is above freezing. Turn the containers a quarter round every time you water to insure even growth from exposure to light and air.

Average house temperature is okay for most herbs and spices. They really appreciate lower temperatures at night, but never down to freezing. Likewise, they can't stand extended periods of excessive heat.

Always keep plants away from drafts of air conditioners or heating systems and far away from any gas appliance.

Pest Control

As with plants grown outdoors, in the event that pests attack herbs grown indoors for cooking or cosmetics, the plants should be washed *only* with a strong spray from a garden hose or immersed and washed in a mild solution of soap and water—not detergent. Herbs that you're not going to eat or use on the skin should be sprayed with malathion, covering both sides of the leaves.

Herb and Spice Propagation

In addition to direct seeding in the outdoor garden as outlined on page 22, there are several methods of starting new plants. Most herbs and spices are prolific and will reseed or put off new shoots for new plants if given half a chance.

Starting Seeds Indoors

To get a headstart on spring you can sow seed indoors weeks before outdoor weather permits. Then when planting time arrives you have transplants ready for the garden or decorative containers. This is a good method for starting perennials that take a long time to germinate. But it's not advisable to start anise, borage, caraway and other plants with long taproots indoors, unless you start them in separate, large containers. Even so, they don't transplant easily and

it is safer to wait and seed them directly in their garden place.

Check individual plant recommendations on pages 36–45 to see what grows easily from seed. Sow them late in winter in nursery flats, trays, or any shallow containers that are clean and have good drainage.

Fill the container to within ½-inch of the top with thoroughly dampened vermiculite. (Some gardeners sow the seed directly into very well-draining soil mix). Mark off rows 2 inches apart and set seeds to the depth and spacing recommended on the seed packet. Gently cover seeds by spreading the surface soil with your hand and pressing. Mist lightly and label the planting. Cover the container with glass or a layer of plastic or enclose in a large plastic bag. Keep at 75°F (24°C) and apply no more water until the first green shows through but open the covering every day for about an hour to let in fresh air.

Take off the plastic cover after germination and move the emerging plants to a place with indirect light (no direct sun) and temperature between 60° and 70°F (16° and 21°C).

When the first true leaves have formed on the seedlings, dig them carefully from the germinating medium and plant them in small containers filled with equal parts of peat moss and vermiculite or other fast-draining soil mix. With a pencil, make a small hole in the new container soil and set in the seedling so its leaves are ½ inch above the surface. Press firmly around the roots and stem and water lightly. Several seedlings can be planted in one pot about 1½ inches apart. Don't forget the labels.

Begin giving the plants as much sunlight as possible, about 12 hours a day, or use fluorescent light burned 16 hours a day and placed about 6 inches over the seedlings. Adjust the light distance as necessary during the growth of the plants. Water the soil carefully to keep just moist.

In a few weeks the plants will need to be transplanted into larger containers where they can remain or be transplanted later into the open garden.

An alternative method is to sow

A greenhouse extension unit in the kitchen window is a handy place to grow a few culinary herbs for inspired cooking. Commercial prefabricated units are reasonably priced. Or construct your own wooden framework, enclose it in glass or heavy plastic and add lightweight wire shelving.

For a quick tabletop garden display, construct a wooden box with inside dimensions sized to hold standard nursery flats, six-packs or small plastic pots (as shown on

page 51). Drill holes in the bottom for drainage. Leave the box natural, seal with wood stain or paint to match the interior design. Simply drop the containers into place and enjoy the young plants indoors.

To propagate cuttings, snip a healthy growing end from a mature herb.

Dip dampened stem into a rooting hormone powder.

Firm growing medium *(above)* and cover with plastic *(below)* for added humidity.

seeds 2 at a time, directly into little cups made of growing medium. Simply drop in the seeds, water thoroughly, place on a tray in a plastic bag and keep at warm room temperature. Remove the bag after seedlings appear. Nurture them along in the same medium or transplant directly into small pots for container gardening. When it's time to plant in the garden, the growing cups can go directly into the ground.

When you transfer indoor seedlings to the garden, give them some kind of protective plastic cover or hotcap during their early stages to shelter them from winds, frost and birds. The cover must have ventilation to keep the plants from overheating during the day.

At the end of the gardening season collect seed from annuals for growing a new batch of plants again in late winter. Store the seed in a cool place or the refrigerator, in an airtight container.

Many of the annuals and biennials will self-seed if you let a few of the plants go. If you live in a cold climate, learn to recognize the emerging seedlings and provide protection to get them started, or take them up and transplant to containers.

Multiply By Dividing

Many indoor and outdoor perennials are best propagated by dividing the plant. Those that grow in clumps such as tarragon, chives and sweet woodruff, need root division every couple of years. Some gardeners divide plants annually; it all depends on how much they grow. You may choose to do this chore in the fall after plants go dormant or in the early spring before there's much new growth.

Dividing is simple:

Just moisten the ground all around and dig the plant up or take it out of its pot. Pull or cut the root clump into sections and replant each section with its foliage into the ground or in containers. Keep soil moist until the plants adjust. If you have an older plant, discard the oldest, compacted center part of the root clump.

Root Cuttings

Thymes, tarragon, lemon balm, sage, rosemary and other plants that send new stems up from their roots can be propagated from root cuttings. Take up pieces of ½-inch diameter roots. Discard the end pieces and cut the remainder into sections about 2 inches long.

Place the pieces of root on top of a flat filled to within an inch of the rim with moist builder's sand or other light growing medium. Cover the root sections with ½ inch of growing medium, water well.

In warm regions encase in clear plastic and set outdoors in the shade. When there's evidence of new growth, remove the protective covering. Set plants out in the garden or in pots when they're several inches high.

In cool climates take the root cuttings in the fall and store them in a cold frame or in a cool covered place until growth appears in the spring. Then transplant them to the garden or individual containers.

Stem Cuttings

A generation ago they were called "slips," today we call them stem cuttings. In either case, rooting cuttings from perennials indoors or out is one of the easiest methods of herbal propagation, often faster than germination from seed. Check pages 36–45 for those that can be propagated this way.

Anytime during the active growing season take cuttings of 4 to 6 inches from healthy foliage growth near the plant tips. To select a good stem, try bending it sharply. The ones that snap off will root best. Cut the 4 to 6 inch length from the plant with a sharp knife or razor blade; make a fresh cut on stems you snap off. Keep the cuttings between layers of dampened paper towel to prevent them from wilting before you can get them into the rooting medium.

Prepare any sort of container that has adequate drainage by filling it with a moistened soilless medium (vermiculite, sand, prepackaged mix or a combination of these).

Take off all foliage from the lower half of the cutting. If desired, dip the cut end in hormone rooting powder to stimulate growth. Poke a hole in the moist medium with a pencil and insert the cutting. Firm it in place. Water well.

Encase the entire cutting and

container in a plastic bag or cover the top of the container with a clear plastic drinking cup to build up humidity. Set it in a warm place where there's indirect light (no bright direct sun). Remove the cover for an hour or so each day to allow fresh air in. When you replace the cover, turn the container to equalize exposure to light.

Rooting may take from one month for tender-stem herbs to several months for woody-stem ones. When the foliage seems to perk up, remove the plastic covering and put the plant in a good growing area.

When the container seems to be filled with roots, transplant to a larger pot or a well-protected spot in the garden. Keep soil moist until new growth gets underway.

Ground Layering

All you have to do to propagate perennials in this method is to help nature along. Many plants layer themselves naturally from branches that come in touch with the soil.

Simply bend a stem where it will touch the earth just below a leaf node and about 12 inches from the growing tip. With a sharp knife scrape slender stems; cut thicker

stems about halfway through. Insert a toothpick, matchstick or a prong of a plastic fork into the cut to wedge it open. Dust either the scraped stem or the wedged cut with hormone rooting powder.

Make a shallow hole directly underneath the branch and mix the soil you've removed with equal parts peat moss and coarse builder's sand. Bend the prepared branch down into the hole and pin it in place with a bent wire loop. Cover with the soil mix, leaving 6 inches of the stem tip exposed. Stake the stem upright. Slowly soak the soil with water and cover the buried section with a stone.

In about 6 weeks carefully remove soil and check to see if any new roots are well-formed. When they're established, cut the stem from the parent just below the new rootball. Transplant the new plant to a container or directly into the garden.

In cold regions, begin the layering early in the spring so the plant will be ready for transplanting in time to establish itself before frost. If this isn't possible and you must do layering in the fall, cover the buried portion with a generous amount of mulch leaving only the tip exposed.

Harvesting Herbs and Spices

For most herb and spice gardeners, the greatest fun comes in the harvest. Snip bits of French tarragon and parsley to add to a simmering dish. Cut a bouquet of yellow tansy flowers to dry for a centerpiece. Pinch leaves of rose geranium to add to sweet sachet or float in finger bowls for a special dinner. Clip a cup of chamomile flowers to brew afternoon tea. Catch the seed from a sesame flower just before it bursts open. Or gather big bunches of sweet marjoram just before it blooms.

Harvesting Through the Season

Most culinary herbs can be used from the time you start thinning the seedlings. The flavor is already there. Snip and clip leaves and sprigs as you need them throughout the growing season. Use scissors, a sharp knife, or your fingernails to take sprigs from a few inches down the stem, just above a set of leaves. Be sure not to take too much growth at once while the plants are young and developing or you may weaken them. Select

Well-planned gardens include an array of herbs to snip all season. Learn proper times to harvest for preservation.

healthy leaves and pluck out yellow or dead ones at the same time to keep the plants continuously groomed.

As you snip and clip you are also determining the shape of the growing plant, so harvest judiciously. You benefit from enjoying the fresh herbs and the plants respond with lusher and fuller growth.

Leaves that are to be eaten fresh as salad greens—rocket, sorrel, borage, burnet, nasturtium —should be gathered when quite young and tender. Old leaves get too tough to eat.

Herbs that send up grassy leaves or stalks directly from the ground—chives and parsley— should be cut just above ground level. Don't just cut off the tops or you'll ruin the plant's appearance and growth habit and the mature growth gets too tough to eat.

Keep an eye out as you pinch through the season. Take out flower buds of tender perennials to increase edible leaf production. If allowed to flower early, these herbs will grow tough as the seeds are set. If you want flowers or seed heads on some plants, let some stems develop through their full cycle. Of course, you'll want to let one or two plants go to seed so they will self-seed the garden or give you seed to harvest and store for planting next season.

Harvesting for Preservation

Sure, you've taken bits and pieces of fresh herbs to use all during the season, but the special harvest is for preserving. With most herbs it comes just when the flowers are about to open and the oils are most heavily concentrated.

Of course, there are exceptions. Sage should be cut when the buds appear and you should wait until the blooms are full to gather hyssop, oregano and thyme. Cut parsley, borage, salad burnet and winter savory when the leaves are young.

Harvest early in the morning after the dew has dried but before the hot sun brings out the oils. Some annuals harvested in early summer may grow enough for a second major harvest provided you don't take too much the first time. In the first harvest, cut them several inches above ground. For fall harvested annuals, cut all the way to the ground.

Lavender, marjoram, rosemary and other shrubby perennials should be cut back to about half the length of the year's growth.

Harvest flowers for drying and fragrances when they are just opened and are fresh looking.

Seed heads are ready when they turn color before they open and scatter their seed on the ground. Harvest heads on a warm, dry day by cutting off the entire head or stem and dropping them into paper bags.

Bring all cut herbs indoors out of the sun as soon as possible after harvesting. Keep the different kinds separated and rinse quickly in cool water to remove dirt. Shake off excess water, drain well, then spread on a flat surface. Pick over and discard bad leaves or petals.

At this point label each bunch. If the garden is cooperative and everything doesn't come at once, harvest and prepare only one or two herbs a day.

Preserving the Herbs

Drying is the time-honored method of preserving most leaves, seeds, and flowers. We offer four variations on the drying theme. A few herbs can be preserved in salt and quite a few take well to freezing. Select the methods that seem best for you and them.

Hang Drying

This old method is still the most colorful way of drying the harvest. All you do is take a bunch of one kind of herb, tie the ends of the stems together with string and hang upside down in a place that's warm, dry and away from direct sunlight. Hang them free where air can circulate all around to prevent mildew. If the room is dusty, place the bunch in a paper bag that's been perforated all around for air circulation. Tie the bag around the stems. This is a good method for drying seed heads: as the seeds fall they are caught in the bottom of the bag.

Depending on the weather, herbs usually take about two weeks to hang dry. They should be crisp and crackly to the touch. Store in labeled jars or bags.

Herbs to be used in cooking should be dried as whole as possible to retain flavor.

Quick Drying

If you want to dry herbs in a hurry, spread the leaves on a cheese-cloth-covered rack in the oven at its lowest temperature. Leave the oven door open and stir the leaves until they are crisp. They'll be ready in a few minutes.

Decorative Drying

To hold the hue in flowers or foliage that you plan to use for decorative purposes, try burying them in a drying medium. The colorful and paper-crisp results can be made into winter bouquets.

You have a choice of several desiccants: household borax powder, fine grained builders' sand, equal parts cornmeal and borax, or—for truer colors—ground or crushed silica gel crystals.

Prepare the freshly picked flowers for drying by cutting off the stems and replacing with lengths of florist's wire pushed through the center of the heads. Wrap the wire around leaf clusters.

Start with a wide-mouthed container that has a tight-fitting lid and pour in about 3 inches of the drying medium. Place the flower or herb sprig upright on top, bending the wire flat. Hold in place while slowly pouring more desiccant all around. Be sure to work the material down in between every petal and leaf to prevent mildew.

Add as many flowers or sprigs as you wish but they must not touch each other. Cover the layer with more desiccant. If you're using a deep container, you can add several layers of bloom or foliage. Cover the top layer with an inch or two of the drying compound.

After the container is filled, put on the lid and store it in a warm, dry place where it can remain undisturbed until the flowers and leaves dry. Most flowers take two to three days. In sand they'll require one to three weeks.

Test the readiness by carefully removing a flower or leaf from the drying box. It should feel dry and crisp. If not completely dried, return it to the box and cover again.

When dry, remove the blooms or sprigs carefully and gently shake or brush off all the desiccant.

To make stems longer, add any desired length of florist's wire and wrap with floral tape, stretching it as you go. Keep out of direct sunlight to hold color longer.

Glycerin-dried rose hips and branches of herbal shrubs such as eucalyptus dramatize winter decorations. The natural color will darken but fragrance remains. The leaves and hips stay soft and supple.

Add one part glycerin (from the drug store) to two parts very hot water. Put into a tightly closed bottle, shake well to mix, then pour into a saucepan and bring just to the boiling point.

Cut or smash the bottom of foliage stems and place in a container. Pour in the hot glycerin mixture until it reaches about two inches up the stems.

Put the container in a warm place with a lot of natural light. Check the container daily. You'll probably need to add more glycerin solution the first few days to keep two inches of stem covered.

If you want to vary the naturally dark brown color that results from the glycerin process, add 1 fluid ounce of food coloring per 3 cups of glycerin solution. The color resulting depends on how long you leave the herb in the mixture.

Normally it takes two to three weeks to complete the preserving. Hips or leaves should be soft and

Tray Drying

For small quantities of herbs or short pieces of stems and seed heads, drying trays are handy. A simple box constructed of 1×1 inch lumber with screen mesh or cheesecloth stapled to the bottom works fine. Make the boxes small enough to hold just a few leaves: 10×10 inches is a good size. Put a 1 inch block at each corner if you want to stack several boxes and still get good air circulation.

Let the leaves stay on stems or strip them off. Make one layer in each tray. Stir the contents gently every few days to assure even drying. Most herbs dry crisp within a week or 10 days according to the weather. Remove from the trays when crisp.

Dry the seed heads the same way, then gently rub the capsules through your hands. A fan on low speed or a natural breeze will blow away the chaff as you drop seed into the tray or a bowl.

shiny after the water and glycerin have been absorbed by the plant. The water evaporates and the glycerin stays behind in the cells.

It's natural for beads of moisture to appear on the surface of the hips or leaves, especially if the air is humid or the material stays too long in solution. When this happens remove from the solution and gently wipe or rinse off the excess moisture. Cut away sticky ends.

Freezing

This method is recommended for a few of the tender herbs including basil, burnet, fennel, tarragon, chives, dill and parsley. Simply tie a small bundle of the herb together and dip it head-first into boiling water for a few seconds. Cool immediately by plunging into ice water for a couple of minutes. (The blanching isn't necessary for basil, chives and dill.) Remove leaves from the stems and put into plastic bags, label and freeze.

Freezing is a good way to save the herbs that you pick and don't use fresh during the season. Just chop the leaves before freezing and store in small bags only as much as you'll use at one time.

Salt Curing

Some of the tender herbs such as basil, burnet, dill, fennel and parsley can be packed down in salt. Wash and drain, remove leaves from their stems, place them in alternate layers with plain table salt in a container, beginning and ending with salt layers. Fill the container completely and cover with an airtight lid. Label and store in a cool dark place.

Packing in Vinegar

The French tightly pack tarragon leaves in little jars, then completely fill the jar with vinegar. You might try this method with other leafy herbs as well.

Preserving Onions

Onions may be frozen, canned, pickled or dried.

To freeze, peel and chop, then store in plastic bags or containers. Use within three months.

To can, peel small onions and boil for 5 minutes in water to which ¾ cup of vinegar has been added. Drain and pack into sterilized jars.

The Shakers traditionally dried bountiful annual harvests of herbs.

Cover with a boiling brine made of ¾ cup vinegar and 3 tablespoons salt to 1 gallon water. Leave ½ inch headscape. Seal and process for 25 minutes in a canner at 10 pounds pressure.

To pickle, follow any pickling recipe: pack, seal and process.

To dry, peel and slice thinly or chop. Spread in a thin layer on a drying rack. Stir daily until crispy. Store in airtight containers.

To dry whole onions, shallots or garlic, simply store in a mesh bag or wire basket. Or make a decorative braid to hang: leave stems on the bulbs and clean off ugly leaves and the first skin layer; braid strands, beginning with three bulbs, just as you would a little girl's pigtails. Continue braiding and adding bulbs. Tie off end with twine. Hang in a dry well-ventilated place. Cut off bulbs and use them as needed.

Preserving Peppers

Peppers may be kept in the same ways as onions.

To freeze, simply wash and halve, remove seeds and pulp. Slice or dice and blanch in boiling water for 2 minutes, if desired. Cool, pack in containers or bags and freeze. Use within three months.

To can, cut out stem ends and remove pulp and seeds. Peel by roasting in a hot oven until skins separate. Chill immediately in cold water. Pack into hot, sterilized jars. Add 1 teaspoon salt and 1 tablespoon lemon juice per quart of boiling water and pour to within ½ inch of jar tops, being sure all the pepper is covered. Seal and process in a canner at 5 pounds pressure for 50 minutes (pints) or 60 minutes (quarts).

To pickle, follow directions in a pickling recipe.

To dry, wash the peppers and remove seeds and pulp, slice into thin strips and blanch in boiling water for 10 minutes. Spread in a thin layer on a drying rack. Stir daily until brittle. Store in airtight containers.

To dry whole, start with heavy twine and tie a square knot around the stem of a whole fresh red, green, or yellow pepper. Continue tying peppers to make a long string. Hang in a dry well-ventilated place. Cut peppers from the string as needed.

Storage and Shelf Life

To retain their flavor, dried herbs should be kept as whole as possible and stored in airtight containers away from the heat of the stove and moisture. Some people advocate dark jars, cans or ceramic containers. Clear jars or bottles— even plastic bags—are equally effective as long as they are kept away from the sun or other bright light.

When stored in a cool ventilated place, leafy herbs can be expected to retain freshness for an entire year. Seeds and roots will keep somewhat longer, depending on the sturdiness of the crop.

Commercially available herbs and spices will last six months or slightly longer before beginning to lose their flavors. They should be stored exactly like homegrown products.

Frozen herbs retain texture and flavor much longer than one might expect. They'll keep indefinitely but are best used within one year. Once they have been thawed, they cannot be refrozen.

Herbal Preservationists

Shaker settlements such as the one at Hancock, Massachusetts (shown on the opposite page and above) have played important roles in the history of herbs. Members of the communal sect have lived closely akin to the earth and its harvests. As a result the Shakers developed new herb varieties, tamed those from the wilds, perfected ways of preserving and encouraged the use of herbs and spices in cooking and crafting.

Herbs and Spices for Home Gardens

Dozens of plants, some of them familiar only as favorite flowers, can be classed as herbs and spices. Select those that are right for your needs and growing conditions.

Thousands of plants that could be classed as herbs and spices are cultivated today. Herbalists often disagree as to which plants should be included in the garden. A few purists insist that only the obvious culinary, fragrance, dye or medicinal plants can be ranked as herbs. Using our definition of herbs and spices as plants that produce useful parts for flavoring, fragrances, decorations or crafts, the plants listed on the following 12 pages reflect the author's selection of herbs and spices suitable to most gardens.

Almost all of the culinary herbs are listed, along with many plants grown for their scents. Some are desirable just for their attractive foliages, flowers or forms. A few ancient herbs are included purely for historical interest. As stated earlier, we choose not to include the strictly medicinal herbs or those that can prove poisonous.

This guide describes the size of specific plants that will be useful in designing and planting the utilitarian landscape. Take note of the light, soil, water and other cultural requirements to help you determine what to plant where.

Gardeners who are new to herbs will probably elect to start with a few common plants and

In addition to orris, other iris relatives are traditional herb companions.

Plant combinations create a living collage of varying textures, leaf forms and shades of green. Here in Susan Fruge's verdant, natural garden in Berkeley, California, nasturtiums spread over several varieties of scented geraniums and a lush mint ground cover.

learn to grow those well before moving on to some that take a little more effort. Don't neglect to select a few that will give drama or color to the garden.

Home gardeners shouldn't expect large harvests from some of these plants. They're included in the list because it will be fun and informative to watch how they grow and contribute to your understanding of the world of herbs and spices. There are many challenges and joys in trying something new, or in the case of many herbs, rediscovering something very old that's been neglected too long by modern gardeners.

Agrimony
(Agrimonia eupatoria)

Also known as cocklebur and church steeples, this 2 to 3 foot high perennial has sets of compound leaves that smell like apricots. A spike of tiny yellow blossoms rises on a hairy stalk in the summer. The flowers turn to a hooked seed pod or cocklebur.

Grow agrimony in any soil that stays dry. It prefers full sun but will adjust to some shade. Propagate from seed or by dividing.

Ajuga
(Ajuga reptans)

Roots of ajuga or bugleweed can be used to make a black dye. The perennial spreads so fast and thickly that it is often used as a ground cover. Shiny oval leaves form flat rosettes with long runners. Varieties are available with foliage of burgundy or green variegated with pink or white. Spiky flowers are in blue, purple, red or white.

Grow this higly adaptable plant in any light or soil conditions. To establish as a ground cover, set plants 6 to 12 inches apart. Propagate by cuttings from the ends of runners.

Alkanet
(Anchusa officinalis)

This biennial herb, known also as bugloss, has rough textured, hairy leaves 3 to 6 inches long. The plant grows to 2 feet and bears clusters of blue to purple flowers that taste like cucumber.

Grow in full sun or partial shade and rich, well-drained soil. Propagate from seed or root division in the spring, or root cuttings in the fall.

Aloe vera
(Aloe barbadensis)

The succulent perennial is a familiar ingredient in cosmetics and skin care products. Very thick succulent leaves usually edged with soft spines grow from 6 to 24 inches. When the plant is old, spikes covered with yellow or red bell flowers may rise from the center.

Aloe survives outdoors only in very mild winter regions. In other areas it should be grown in containers placed where the temperature does not drop below 50° F (10° C). Pot in any standard houseplant soil mix. Let the soil dry out between waterings, especially in the winter. After the first year, fertilize annually with half-strength houseplant food. Propagate by planting the suckers that form around the base in moist sand.

Angelica
(Angelica species)

Only two species of angelica are of interest to home gardeners. Both are biennial members of the carrot family with large, light green leaves and showy clusters of white or greenish flowers on hollow stems. *A. archangelica* grows 4 to 6 feet and is aromatic and celerylike.

Similar is *A. atropurpurea,* except the stems and veins of the leaves are purple. Other species of angelica are weedy or poisonous.

Grow in partial shade and well-drained, lightly moist soil. Propagate by seeds.

Anise
(Pimpinella anisum)

Licorice-flavored leaves and seed characterize this slow-growing annual. There are tiny umbrella-like clusters of yellowish blooms. Oval leaves at the base change into three-segment leaves higher up the 18 to 24 inch stems.

Grow anise in full sun and fairly rich, well-drained soil. Propagate by seed. Don't transplant after established. Difficult in north because of long growing season; start early indoors and leave in pots when carried outside.

Artemisia
(Artemisia species)

Several species are grown for their feathery foliages. In

addition to tarragon (*A. dracunculus),* listed separately, two species are important to the herbalist.

Wormwood (*A. absinthium),* one of the Biblical bitter herbs, was used to flavor absinthe liqueur. It is highly decorative with deep-cut silvery leaves covered with grey downy hairs. Grows 2 to 4 feet in height and bears yellowish flowers in summer.

Southernwood (*A. abrotanum*) has lemon-scented, feathery green foliage. The woody perennial grows 3 to 4 feet in height. Flowers are yellowish.

Grow artemisias in full sun and dry soil. Propagate from divisions or stem cuttings.

Basil
(Ocimum basilicum)

The silky leaves of this bushy annual look creased. Grows to 2 feet. Sprinkles of whitish to lavender flowers. One variety (*O.b.* 'Dark Opal') has vivid purple leaves. Bush basil (*O. minimum*) is more compact. Keep all basils pinched for fuller growth. Do not fertilize.

Basils grow best in full sun or partial shade. They prefer moderately rich soil that is kept lightly moist. Propagate by seed.

Bay
(Laurus nobilis)

Sweet bay is an evergreen shrub that will grow into a medium-sized tree under favorable conditions. The 2 to 4-inch shiny, dark green leaves are used in flavoring many dishes. The plant produces small yellow flowers followed by black or purple berries.

Seeds take so long to germinate and cuttings don't always root, that it's best to start with a nursery plant. Pot in a container that is comfortable for the rootball. Use any well-drained soil mix. Let the soil dry out a little between waterings. Grow in bright light with some shade during the hot part of the summer day; in a cool room in winter.

Bayberry
(Myrica pensylvanica)

A deciduous or semi-evergreen with gray berries that yield a wax used in candlemaking, bayberry is a native American shrub. Grows to 9 feet, with dull green aromatic leaves to 4 inches.

The shrub grows best in poor, sandy soil. Keep as many roots together as possible when transplanting.

Bedstraw
(Galium verum)

The stems and leaves of this perennial were once grown to stuff mattresses, thus its common name. Today it is grown for ornamental purposes. Tiny yellow flowers cluster on stems from 1 to 3 feet. Leaves are mossy and circle the stems in groups of six to eight.

Plant bedstraw in full sun or partial shade; routine garden maintenance. The sprawly plant looks best when staked. Propagate from seed or division.

Bergamot
(Monarda didyma)

Bee balm and Oswego tea are other common names for this perennial that was the tea substituted by rebellious Boston patriots during the tea boycott. It grows 3 feet tall and produces shaggy, flaming red flowers that are quite aromatic. Wild bergamot or horsemint *(M. punctata)* is grown for the minty leaves used in tea and fragrances.

Bergamot doesn't grow well where the winters are warm and humid. It tolerates some shade but prefers full sun. Grows in humus-rich soil that's kept fairly moist. It's slow to start from seed, so buy nursery stock or propagate by division. Cut back flower heads the first year before they bloom to increase strength in the plant. Roots are very shallow, so exercise care in weeding. Prune almost to the ground in the fall.

Borage
(Borago officinalis)

A highly ornamental annual or biennial, borage grows to a height of 1 to 3 feet. Gray-green leaves set off star shaped, bright blue flowers. Requires lots of garden space Does not transplant well. Sow 3 times at 4-week intervals to stretch fresh harvest. Borage grows in full sun or partial shade and adapts to any soil, but rfers it on the poor side. Water moderately and allow soil to dry a bit. Propagate by seed.

Boxwood
(Buxus species)

Though not itself a herb, boxwood has become an indispensable part of the formal herb garden. The evergreen shrubs are used as borders and hedges to define patterns. Although boxwood will grow large in mild climates, in the herb garden it's kept small and compact through regular clipping. Once established the plants live for many years. There are gardens that have plants started during the American colonial period.

Common boxwood *(B. sempervirens)* has dark green, glossy leaves that are about 1½ inches long. The variety 'Suffruticosa' is a dwarf that's often used in the herb garden. If you live in cold climates, your best bet is the Japanese boxwood *(B. microphylla)*, especially the variety *koreana*.

Boxwoods tolerate partial shade and need well-drained soil. Prune after new growth has formed in late spring. Keep dead leaves and twigs cut out from the inside. Propagate by cuttings or division.

Burnet
(Poterium sanguisorba)

Too often overlooked, burnet is a perennial with rounded, toothed leaves that stay rather close to the ground. Flower stems rise above the leaves to a height of 2 feet. Flowers are unusual looking and rose colored.

Plant burnet in full sun and well-drained soil that's kept fairly dry. Propagate from seed or division.

To grow burnet as a container plant or ground cover, keep the flower shoots cut back. Eat the leaves when young and tender.

Calendula
(Calendula officinalis)

Shakespeare and ancient herbalists called them marigolds. Now they're known mostly by their botanical name or as pot-marigolds. Calendulas enjoy a long

flowering season. In warm regions they bloom in winter and spring; elsewhere in summer and fall. The annual has angular, branched, hairy stems to 2 feet with 4 inch orange flowers. Hybrids range from pale yellow to deep orange.

Most gardeners start with transplants from the nursery. Grow in full sun and ordinary soil. Care is routine. Propagate from seed.

Caper Bush
(Capparis spinosa)

Pickled flower buds of the caper bush are the familiar capers known to good cooks. The plant is a spiny shrub that tends to straggle. In warm regions grow the plant outdoors. In most places it needs the warmth of a greenhouse to produce usable buds.

Caraway
(Carum carvi)

This biennial propagates easily. Carrot-like leaves grow to 15 inches the first year. Sturdy shoots to 2 feet are topped with white umbel flowers the second year. Doesn't transplant well because of long taproot.

Grow in full sun and well-drained soil. Propagate by seed.

Carnations and Pinks
(Dianthus species)

The clovelike fragrance of carnations and pinks has kept them among the ranks of herb and spice garden plants through the centuries. Sizes range from low-growing miniature pinks with small flowers to the tall florist's carnation. Flowers come in every shade of pink and red, as well as white. The carnation species *(D. caryophyllus)* also comes in shades of yellow, orange, lavender and purple. Both pinks and carnations come with striped and variegated petals. The evergreen foliage is often gray-blue.

Most dianthus species are perennial. All need full sun, although some will bloom in partial shade. Soil should be well-drained and slightly alkaline. The carnation species is most successful in warmer climates or as a greenhouse plant.

Catnip
(Nepeta cataria)

Felines love the 2 to 3 foot perennial. Heart shaped leaves have toothed edges. White or lavender flower spikes grow in midsummer. Cut back each year to avoid a straggly appearance. Protect seedlings from cats until well established.

Catnip grows in either full sun or partial shade and light, rich soil. Keep evenly moist. Propagate by seed, cuttings or division.

Chamomile
(Chamaemelum nobile)

A carpet or walkway of fragrant chamomile is an herb garden tradition. This evergreen perennial forms a soft spreading mat of fine foliage about 3 inches high and 12-inch high, small daisylike flowers dot the plant in summer. They make a delicious tea.

To establish chamomile, start from seed or buy little plants. Set in full sun or partial shade in light, well-drained but moist soil. If you need to confine this fast-

spreader, sink header boards around the area to a depth of 6 inches. If grown as a ground cover, occasional clippings with a mower will keep it controlled and lush.

For container gardening, plant in a large flat tray. Propagate by seed and division in the spring.

Chervil
(Anthriscus cerefolium)

This sweet aromatic annual grows to 2 feet. Fernlike foliage turns pink in fall. Tiny white flowers grow in clusters. Seedlings are difficult to transplant. Will self-seed if allowed to flower.

Grow in filtered shade and fairly rich soil that's kept slightly moist. Propagate by seed.

Chinese Chives
(Allium tuberosum)

Known also as *gow choy, chung fa* or *yuen sai,* this pungent version of chives is prolific. The spring crop will reappear in the fall if plants are left to reseed themselves. Grow in full sun or partial shade in well-drained soil. Propagate from seed.

Chives
(Allium schoenoprasum)

Chives are perennial herbs that grow in clumps with slim grasslike leaves to 10 inches. Refrain from snipping only the growing tips as in most other herbs. Becomes tough unless clipped close to ground several times during season.

Chives prefer full sun and rich soil, but tolerate partial shade and a lighter soil mix. Keep fairly moist. Propagate by seed or division.

Chrysanthemum
(Chrysanthemum coronarium)

Both the young leaves and flower heads of garland chrysanthemum or crown daisies are used to flavor oriental dishes. The plant grows from 1 to 3 feet tall with flowers of yellow shading to white.

Give it the routine care of annual flowers in the garden. Propagate from seeds.

Citrus
(Citrus species)

Both the flowers and fruits of citrus plants are valued by herb and spice gardeners. Dwarf varieties of lemons, limes and oranges can be grown in containers for easy winter protection in most regions. Greenhouse gardeners discover citrus plants to be adaptable and productive. Subtropical gardeners can add the plants to the outdoor garden.

Grow in full sun and slightly acid soil that is well-drained. Provide additional humidity when growing in containers. Prune in early spring to maintain desirable size and shape. Propagate from seed or cuttings.

Coffee
(Coffea arabica)

Expect a good experience but not a crop from growing the coffee tree at home. Prune its growing tips to develop a compact shrub or small tree with glossy, dark green leaves. Spring brings fragrant white flowers followed by bright red beans in the summer.

Grow coffee in bright indirect light. Keep above 60° F (16° C) in winter and treat as you would other indoor houseplants. If leaves yellow, feed with acid-type fertilizer. Propagate from seed or tip cuttings.

Columbine
(Aquilegia species)

Among the most decorative plants in the herb garden are the columbines now grown for their showy flowers in spring and summer. The delicate blooms with prominent spurs are borne in purples, blues, reds, yellows, pinks and white. Foliage is blue-green and lacy. The 1½ to 3 foot perennial

is long lived once established in the garden.

The European columbine *(A. vulgaris)* is the most frequently grown. For the rock garden try the alpine columbine *(A. alpina),* a smaller plant that needs protection. Several species are on preservation lists in the United States and cannot be dug from the wilds. Most garden catalogues offer a good selection of columbines.

Plant in full sun and well-drained soil. To prolong blooming period, keep pods picked as they fade. Propagate by seeds or root divisions. Flowers of self-propagated seedlings are usually inferior and you'll probably want to pull them up when they appear.

Comfrey
(Symphytum officinale)

Known also by the colorful names knit-bone and blackwort, comfrey is a perennial that grows as tall as 3 feet.

Large hairy leaves measure up to 20 inches. Comfrey produces a long season of blooms in white, yellow, mauve or blue. Keep the flowers cut to encourage more leaf growth.

The plant prefers full sun, but will tolerate partial shade. Grow in fairly rich soil that's kept moist. Propagate from root cuttings or divisions.

Coriander
(Coriandrum sativum)

This annual grows quickly 12 to 30 inches high. Oval leaves with serrated edges along main stems; feathery leaves on side branches. Flowers bloom in parasol shaped clusters of pinkish white. If you want only leaves, known as cilantro or Chinese parsley, sow seeds every two weeks for continuous supply.

Plant in full sun or partial shade and moderately rich, well-drained soil. Propagate by seed.

Costmary
(Chrysanthemum balsamita)

Also known as alecost and bibleleaf, this weedy perennial has 7-inch leaves with toothed edges. Erect flower stems grow to 4 feet. Cut back leggy stems for fuller plants.

Costmary can be grown in full sun or partial shade and any well-drained soil. Propagate by division.

Cumin
(Cuminum cyminum)

Seeds of cumin plants are collected for their pungent flavor. The plant is good for edging as it grows to only 6 inches in height. Small pink or white blooms turn to tiny seed.

Plant cumin in full sun and well-drained soil. It must have at least three months of hot weather to mature. If the climate is cold, start seed indoors to get a head start. Propagate from seed.

Dandelion
(Taraxacum officinale)

The challenge here is learning to think of dandelion as a useful part of the garden, not just a lawn weed. Confine dandelion to raised beds and your attitude towards it as a pest may vanish.

Leaves of the newer cultivated varieties are tastier than the wild form and many seed companies offer them. Remember the whole plant is edible—roots, leaves, stems and flowers.

It's a cool weather crop and can be planted for very early picking and again for fall harvest. During hot summer weather produces tough foliage.

Delphinium and Larkspur
(Delphinium and *Consolida* species)*

The delphiniums and larkspurs deserve a prominent place in the large herb garden strictly for their richly colored flower spires. Larkspurs *(Consolida ambigua* and *orientalis,* often sold as *Delphinium ajacis)* are popular annuals with flower spikes 1 to 3 feet high in purple, blue, pink or white. Foliage is feathery.

Common delphinium—candle or bee larkspur *(D. elatum)*—is a perennial that grows to 6 feet with magnificent flower spires in blue, purple, lavender, pink, white, as well as combinations of these hues. Other interesting perennial delphiniums include garland larkspur *(D. x belladona),* Chinese Larkspur *(D. grandiflorum),* and the western orange-red larkspur *(D. nudicaule).*

Grow in full sun and very well-drained soil. All delphinium species require heavy feeding and need stakes to support the top-heavy flowers. To assure a second round of blooms, cut flowers before they can set seed. They're pretty when dried. Propagate larkspurs from seeds, delphiniums from seeds, rooted stock or division. Delphiniums do not always grow successfully in areas with mild winters or extremes of heat or drought. Larkspurs grow everywhere.

Dill
(Anethum graveolens)

Familiar annual with light green feathery foliage grows to height of 2 to 4 feet. Tiny greenish yellow flowers form in parasol shaped clusters atop stems. Doesn't transplant well. Self-seeds easily.

Full sun is essential for dill. Any well-drained soil proves satisfactory. Propagate by seed.

Dittany of Crete
(Origanum dictamnus)

White, wooly haired leaves cover this perennial that grows to 1 foot. Long-lasting flower bracts support tiny pinkish blooms.

This ancient herb needs full sun and well-drained soil. Propagate by seed, stem cuttings or root division.

Elecampane
(Inula helenium)

Bright yellow sunflowerlike blooms are produced on this shrubby perennial that grows to a height of 4 to 6 feet. Narrow leaves to 18 inches cover the plant.

Grow in full sun and ordinary garden soil that's kept moist.

Fennel, Sweet
(Foeniculum vulgare)

A tender perennial that's grown as an annual, sweet fennel reaches 3 to 5 feet with bright green hollow stems. It has narrow feathery leaves and flat clusters of golden flowers. Sow seeds in place in the garden or in large containers as fennel doesn't transplant well. Grow in full sun and light, well-drained soil. Propagate by seed.

Fennel Flower
(Nigella sativa)

Spicy seeds that smell like nutmeg are produced in late summer by this annual, known also as black cumin or love-in-a-mist. It's a welcome addition to the herb garden with delicate foliage that resembles sweet fennel, but isn't a relative. Small blue or white flowers top each stem in summer, fol-

lowed by the seed pods.

Plant nigella in full sun and well-drained soil. Since it produces only a few seeds, plant generously. Propagate from seed. Sow in place as it doesn't transplant successfully.

Foxglove
(Digitalis purpurea)

No plant in the herb garden is more spectacular than foxglove. The flower spikes tower to 5 feet and are lined with trumpet blossoms of pure white, through yellows, pinks and reds, to purple. Foxglove is a hardy biennial and blooms don't appear until the second year. Cutting back in early summer often will encourage second blooms late in the season.

The plant was important in early herb gardens for the digitalis obtained as a medication. Today it's grown for its beauty.

Plant in full sun or partial shade in well-drained soil. Routine garden care is sufficient. Protect the plants during the first winter with a mulch. Propagate from seed.

The plant is not recommended for areas with high summer humidity.

Garlic
(Allium sativum)

The familiar garlic is a perennial bulb that reaches a height of 2 to 3 feet. Long narrow leaves sheath the flower stalk topped by clusters of white or lavender blooms. Bulbs multiply during season into clusters of bulblets or cloves.

Garlic needs full sun and rich, well-drained soil. Propagate by dividing the bulbs.

Gas Plant
(Dictamnus albus)

Among the most curious events in nature is the vapor produced by this

perennial in hot weather that will burst into flame when ignited. Also known as burning bush and false dittany, it is a bushy plant that grows to a height of 2 feet. Leaves are dark and leathery and arranged in pairs. Very delicate pinkish or white blooms with reddish filaments and green anthers begin appearing when the plant is a few years old.

Gas plant tolerates partial shade but prefers full sun. Prepare well-drained soil deep for its extensive root system. Provide routine plant maintenance. Don't be dismayed when plant dies down in late fall; like most other perennial herbs it will come back each spring. Propagate from seed.

Geraniums, Scented
(Pelargonium species)

Among the most fragrant of all the plants in the herb garden are the scented geraniums. These tender shrubby plants grow from 2 to 4 feet. Scents are released by hot sun on the leaves or by touching them. Foliages come in a variety of forms, from small delicate fernlike leaves to quite large rounded ones, in many shades of green, some with variegations. The flowers of most are small but colorful in shades of rose.

The numerous varieties include the following scents: Almond *(P. quercifolium);* Apple *(P. odoratissimum);* Apricot and strawberry *(P. scabrum);* Lemon *(P. crispum, P. x limoneum);* Lime *(P. nervosum);* Nutmeg *(P. x fragrans);* Peppermint *(P. tomentosum);* Rose *(P. capitatum, P. graveolens).*

Give the scented geraniums the advantage of full

sun. They enjoy light well-drained soil that stays slightly dry. However, if too dry, they will shed their lower leaves. Plants in containers need one-half strength fertilizer every two weeks when flowering, monthly during the rest of the year.

Although many scented geraniums have a tendency to get leggy, pinching the growing tips will help train the plants to grow bushier and fuller. Propagate by root cuttings and stem cuttings.

Germander
(Teucrium chamaedrys)

Herbalists value germander as a ground cover or edging for formal designs. The perennial grows in clumps from 6 to 18 inches tall and spreads easily along creeping roots. Leaves are dark green, shiny ovals with scalloped edges. Summer flowers appear in pink whorls where leaves join the stems.

Grow in full sun or partial shade and well-drained, fairly rich soil. Spring pruning keeps the plants bushy and lush. Propagate from stem cuttings, root divisions or seed.

Ginger
(Zingiber officinale)

The showy source of ginger root is a 3 to 4 feet high bushy plant with long leafstalks. Flowers are grown in a conelike cluster of bracts that overlap. In its natural tropical environment the stalks wither after about 10 months and the roots or rhizomes are dug up.

Grow outdoors in summer months or year round as a containerized indoor or greenhouse plant.

To start a ginger plant obtain fresh roots from the market or Oriental food shop. Plant roots with the

sprout end up and eyes just above soil. Use rich, moist soil in a pot (or in the ground if you live where summer days are hot). Ginger needs good drainage, lots of sun and humidity. Protect it from high winds and low temperatures.

After the plant matures it will grow new sprouts out of the ground in front of it. Dig up one of these sprouts and you'll find a tender new growth of root with a much subtler, fresher taste than the supermarket roots.

The young sprouts of the plant are also edible and prized by Chinese and Japanese cooks.

Good-King-Henry
(Chenopodium bonus-henricus)

The large arrowhead leaves of Good-King-Henry or English mercury are often eaten as a substitute for spinach. The perennial grows to a height of 30 inches with yellowish blooms at the end of the leafstalk.

Plant the herb in partial shade and well-drained soil. Feed with any balanced fertilizer to promote growth and refrain from harvesting many leaves until the third year. Propagate by root division.

Early shoots are sometimes eaten as asparagus substitute. Cover them with leaf mold as they grow to blanch white and tender.

Heliotrope
(Heliotropium arborescens)

Let your nose be your guide at the nursery in choosing varieties of this half-hardy shrub for the garden. While most have delightful vanilla-like fragrances, a few have no scent. Plants grow from 1 to 3 feet or more and must be pinched back to

keep them bushy, beginning when they are only 4 or 5 inch seedlings. Tiny flowers appear in clusters from white to dark purple with shades of rose and lavender in between.

Grow heliotrope in full sun, in a rich soil that's kept moist at all times. Indoor or greenhouse container-grown plants may be subject to aphids and red spider mites. Propagate by seed.

Hens-and-Chickens
(Sempervivum tectorum)

This succulent perennial, also known as houseleek, has been grown with other herbs through the centuries. The superstitious uses have faded but the plant retains popularity due to the attractive shape. Thick leaves form a rosette that produces small offshoots around the base. The mother plant dies when flower shoots appear from the center. Young plants continue to grow.

Houseleeks need full sun and very fast-draining soil. Let the soil go nearly dry during winter months while the plant rests. Propagate by removing the small offshoots.

Hollyhock/Marsh Mallow
(Alcea rosea)/(Althaea officinalis)

Towering hollyhocks are among the most impressive planting in any garden. Flower spikes 5 to 8 feet tall are covered with blooms in many shades of pink, red, yellow and white. The plants are biennials but self-sow so freely that they're usually treated as perennials.

The look-alike marsh mallow is a perennial that has long been associated with herb gardening. Its flower spikes grow only to 4 feet with small pink flowers.

Plant both in full sunlight and well-drained soil. Marsh mallows prefer fairly wet soil. Spider mites are especially fond of the species, so be on your guard and keep the malathion handy. Propagate by seeds or division.

Horehound
(Marrubium vulgare)

Velvety leaves and downy stems characterize this hardy perennial. Small white flowers that attract bees are produced along the stems in late summer.

Plant horehound in full sun and poor soil that remains on the dry side. Propagate from seed.

Horseradish
(Armoracia rusticana)

The pungent roots of horseradish are important additions to the culinary garden. The tall plant has glossy green leaves and profuse small white flowers. It's a hardy perennial but best treated as an annual.

To keep the plant from spreading as a weed and to assure quality roots, in the spring make a mound of soil 2 feet high by 2 feet wide and as long as you need. Cut the roots into 9-inch sections and plant them in the side of the mound, spaced 12 inches apart and 12 to 18 inches above normal ground level. Position them on a slant, small end down and large end 2 to 3 inches below soil surface.

After the leaves get about 12 inches high, push back the soil above the cuttings and remove all but 1 or 2 of the crown sprouts. Rub off the small roots that have started from the sides of the cuttings but be sure not to disturb the branch roots at the base. Re-cover the root with soil. If you want a really great horseradish, repeat this operation in about four weeks. Delay harvest until October or November. Keep soil nicely moist throughout the growing season.

Hyssop
(Hyssopus officinalis)

This compact, shrubby perennial stays under 2 feet tall. Smooth narrow leaves grow opposite on woody stems with spikes of white, pink or blue flowers. Good in landscape. A look-alike relative, the giant or anise hyssop *(Agastache foeniculum)*, grows larger.

Plant hyssop in full sun and well-drained soil slightly on the alkaline side. Propagate by seed, stem cuttings or root division.

Jasmine
(Jasminum species)

Fragrant blossoms make these erect or climbing shrubs a delight to the herb and spice gardener. Most have small, shiny dark green leaves. Flowers in yellow or white appear in clusters at axils or tips.

Put them in the sun and keep the soil lightly moist.

Varieties of *J. sambac* like warmth and are good indoor plants. Propagate by cuttings of nearly mature wood.

Johnny-Jump-Up
(Viola tricolor)

Miniature pansy or heart's ease is a charming little plant to add to the herb garden. It's a self-seeding biennial that grows about 6 to 8 inches high. Leaves vary from feathery to heart shaped on the same stem. The flowers are tricolored in purple, yellow and white, and bloom all through spring and summer.

Plant the little viola in full sun and any soil that's kept moist but never soggy. Propagate from seed but don't expect blooms until the second year. If you're in a hurry, set out nursery transplants.

Lamb's Ear
(Stachys byzantina)

The soft fuzzy foliage looks like the common name implies. Wooly hairs cover the 3-to-6 inch gray-green leaves. Thick flower stalks appear early in the summer.

Lamb's ear make an effective ground cover. To establish, plant about 12 to 15 inches apart in full sun and well-drained soil. Every two or three years, divide root clumps to avoid overcrowding. Propagate slowly from seed or more efficiently from divisions.

Lavender
(Lavandula species)

Long-time favorite perennials, lavenders are woody stemmed and grow from 1½ to 4 feet. Fragrant blooms are produced in lavender to deep purple. Leaves can be bright green to gray. English lavender *(L. spica)* is the most widely grown species.

Lavender requires full sun and very fast-draining soil. Keep on the dry side. Propagate from seed or stem cuttings.

Leek
(Allium ampeloprasum)

A hardy member of the onion family, the leek looks like a fattened green onion with much larger leaves and practically no swelling of the bulb.

Leeks need deep soil and plenty of water and fertilizer. Plant them in trenches 4 to 6 inches deep and pile up soil around the stems as they grow to produce the long white edible. Since it is difficult to prevent particles of soil from getting in between the leaves and causing grittiness when eaten, some gardeners wrap corrugated cardboard around the stems before earthing them up. Start leeks from seed or transplants.

Lemon Balm
(Melissa officinalis)

This lemon-scented plant spreads much as the mint family does. A perennial also known as sweet balm, it has plenty of green leaves that grow to a height of 2 to 3 feet. There are small clusters of inconspicuous white flowers in summer.

Lemon balm responds best to full sun and relatively poor soil that's kept dry. Propagate from seed or division.

Lemon Verbena
(Aloysia triphylla)

The delightfully lemonlike fragrance of the leaves is sufficient reason to grow this shrub. Sometimes sold as *Lippia citriodora*, the plant grows to 10 feet in height. Pale green leaves in groups of three or four are usually deciduous or sometimes evergreen.

Give the plant full sun and routine garden care. It's successful as a container plant indoors or out. Provide winter protection to keep the plant evergreen. Propagate by new growth cuttings.

Lovage
(Levisticum officinale)

A celery look-alike, lovage grows to heights of 3 to 7 feet, then the perennial dies back to the ground in winter. Summer blooms of greenish flowers ripen into seeds.

Grow in full sun or partial shade and rich soil that's kept evenly moist. Lovage needs winter freezing temperatures and is difficult in warm coastal areas. Propagate from just-ripened seed or root divisions.

Marjoram
(Origanum majorana)

A perennial grown as an annual, marjoram reaches 1 to 2 feet in height. The small oval leaves are light green on top, grey-green underneath and covered with fine hair. Flowers form in tight clusters of white to lilac.

Grow in full sun and slightly alkaline soil. Keep lightly moist. Propagate by seed, cuttings, or layering.

Mint
(Mentha species)

The mints are all fast growing, spreading perennials. Like common peppermint *(M. x piperita)*, they have square stems and opposite aromatic leaves. All mints are grown alike.

Stiff stems of the pineapple mint *(M. suaveolens)* grow 20 to 30 inches. The green, rounded leaves are slightly hairy. Small purplish white flowers are produced on 2- to 3-inch spikes.

Orange bergamot *(M. piperita var. citrata)* grows from 1 to 2 feet and spreads rapidly. Stems are reddish green, oval leaves are edged in purple. Light purple flowers bloom in uppermost axils. Leaves have citrus odor when crushed.

Pennyroyal *(M. pulegium)* is characterized by small oval hairy leaves on creeping stems to 2 feet in length. Lavender-blue or pink flowers grow in tiers on 6- to 12-inch-long flower spikes.

The mint jelly herb spearmint *(M. spicata)* grows to

a height of 1 to 2 feet with reddish stems and crinkly pointed leaves. Flower spikes of 2 to 4 inches are lavender in color.

All mints thrive in partial shade and moderately rich soil that is kept lightly moist. Keep roots under control with sunken header boards or plant in underground pots. Cut flowering stalks before they go to seed. Propagate by stem cuttings, root division or layering.

Myrtle
(Myrtus communis)
Varieties of this highly aromatic evergreen shrub grow from 3 to 10 feet tall, or more under ideal conditions. Small shiny leaves, tiny fragrant flowers and peppery berries characterize the plant. Myrtle is popular in formal gardens because it can be pruned to almost any form.

Grow in full sun or partial shade and well-drained soil. In very warm climates myrtle can be grown outdoors all year, in other areas it must be a container plant and moved into a protected winter location. Propagate from seed, cuttings of half-ripened wood or by layering.

Nasturtium
(Tropaeolum species)
Peppery tasting flowers of this climbing annual make colorful additions to summer salads. Leaves are also edible and the buds and seeds can be pickled as substitutes for capers. Flowers have spurs and appear in orange, yellow, red, creamy white, salmon and deep mahogany.

Grow nasturtium in full sun and well-drained soil. If the soil is too rich or you overfeed, there'll be lots of lush foliage but few flowers.

Watch for aphids that seem to thrive on nasturtiums. Propagate from seed.

Nasturtiums will grow indoors in bright sunlight or under artificial lighting. Keep the temperature cool. Feed with half-strength houseplant fertilizer monthly if you want flowers.

Onions
(Allium cepa)
Members of the onion family are indispensable in the culinary herb and spice garden. They produce interesting little blooms that are good for drying. Also see leeks (page 41) and garlic (page 39).

Any variety of the standard onion can be a "green onion" or "scallion" if harvested when the bulb is small. However, 'White Lisbon' is the variety most widely grown for this purpose. There are also several

varieties known as bunching onions that do not produce bulbs and are eaten as green onions.

Fully developed onions are harvested when the tops begin to yellow and fall over. They're sun dried for a few days and stored in cool, dry well-ventilated places for months.

Varieties are classed as long-day and short-day crops and come in white, yellow and red bulbs. For the pearl or pickling onions, plant variety 'Eclipse' thickly in the spring and harvest when quite young.

Egyptian onions produce clusters of small red bulblets and hollow stalks.

Shallots, prized by gourmets, are multiplier onions that divide into clumps of small bulbs. They're harvested and dried just as standard onions are.

Grow onions in plenty

of sunlight and well-drained soil. If your season is short, start with transplants instead of seeds or sets.

Oregano
(Origanum vulgare)

This tender perennial is a close relative of sweet marjoram but has a sharper flavor. It grows shrublike to 2½ feet with broad oval leaves that are dark green. Flowers are pale pinkish. Replace container-grown plants when they get woody.

Grow in full sun and well-drained soil. Keep lightly moist. Propagate from seed, cuttings or root division.

Orris
(Iris x germanica florentina)
Sweet scented roots of the German or Florentine iris have been valued by herbalists for many centuries. Swordlike leaves grow to 2 feet high with large white flowers that are veined with blue and marked with yellow beards. Other iris relatives are also traditionally grown with herbs.

Spring-blooming iris require full sun and the typical well-drained soil of other herbs. Cut flowers after fading to prevent seed formation that weakens bulb or rhizome growth. Foliage will die back in fall. Dig bulbs up every few years after flowering. Replant some to propagate. When planting place the rhizomes just below soil surface in horizontal position with roots downward. Peel and dry rhizomes in the sun to use in herbal fragrances.

Parsley
(Petroselinum crispum)
Parsley is a biennial but is usually planted annually. It has very dark green leaves that are deeply curled. The

Italian variety *(P. c. neapolitanum)* has flat, broad leaves. Gets off to a slow start, sometimes hard to germinate. Soak seed 24 hours before planting. Easiest from nursery transplants.

Parsley prefers partial shade. Keep moderately rich soil fairly moist. Propagate from seed.

Peppers
(Capsicum species)
The familiar green or red pepper is unrelated to the black and white peppercorn spice of the Far East. You have a big choice in the degree of hotness to plant in the garden, from sweet mild peppers that are ground into paprika to the hot Tabasco-type pepper that is rarely grown at home. For chili choose from the following varieties: 'Red Chili,' 'Long Red Cayenne,' 'Hungarian Wax,' and 'Chili Jalapeno.' All are hot and can be dried, then ground for spicing many dishes.

Peppers need hot weather to set bloom but daytime temperatures over 90° F (32° C) will also cause the blossoms to drop; so will night temperatures much below 60° F (16° C).

Peppers are easiest to start as transplants from a nursery, or grow your own transplants indoors. Do not transplant into the garden until weather is quite warm. Keep peppers well watered, especially at flowering time when you should give them a light application of fertilizer.

Peppers make attractive container plants, especially small-fruited hot varieties. They prove successful indoors, even under lights. Outdoors peppers are colorful additions to the flower beds or herbaceous borders.

Rocket
(Eruca vesicaria sativa)

This weedy annual is known to the French as *roquette*. The Greeks call it *roka* and the Italians *aragula*. It's a low-growing plant that looks like mustard with white, yellow or purple edible flowers. The young leaves have a horseradish flavor.

Grow rocket in full sun just as you would other plants with edible greens. It's a cool weather crop and becomes bitter in hot summer. Propagate from seed.

Rosemary
(Rosmarinus officinalis)

This old favorite is a not-quite-winter-hardy ever-green. Grows between 2 and 6 feet in height. Except in mild winter climates it should be grown in mov-

able containers so it can winter over in a cool, frost-free place. Leaves are needlelike, glossy green over grey-green. Blooms in clusters of lavender to blue.

Grow in full sun and well-drained soil. Keep fairly dry. Propagate by seed, cuttings or half-ripened wood or layering.

Roses
(Rosa species)

If you've ever been high on the aroma of one of the old roses, chances are you've already added one to your garden. The fragrances are heavy and lingering. Old roses are easy to grow, quite hardy and very pest free. The petals may be delicately single or heavily double and come mostly in shades of pink, rose and white, with a few yellows.

The foliage of the sweet-briers (*R. rubiginosa,* also known as *R. eglanteria*) is reminiscent of ripe apples. Damask roses (*R. damascena* and *R. x bifera*) are the

source of attar of roses used in perfumes. Moss roses are covered with a soft mossy growth over the calyx and stem that leaves a sticky, fragrant resin on your fingers.

Other roses to consider that blend well with herbs and provide fragrant petals for cooking and crafts include the apothecary's rose (*R. gallica officinalis*), the cabbage rose (*R. centifolia*), tea rose (*R. odorata*), hybrid perpetuals, noisettes and hybrid musks. Rugosa roses are valued for their large hips, full of vitamin C.

Plant roses in as much sun as possible in well-drained rich soil. You can't give roses too much water as long as the drainage is good. Unlike the modern roses, one feeding in the early spring is enough for most old species. Propagate by stem cuttings.

Safflower
(Carthamus tinctorius)

Also known as false saffron, the annual safflower grows from 1 to 2 feet high with spiny green leaves. Orange flowers resemble thistles. Tiny orange-red florets are dried in separate piles to produce red or golden yellow powder, sometimes used as substitute for true saffron but more importantly in dyes.

Plant in light soil in a warm sunny location. Grows best in dry summer climates without a lot of rainfall.

Saffron
(Crocus sativus)

You'll have to grow a lot of flowers in order to gather enough golden saffron for spicing. But the little fall crocus blooms are so pretty you might not mind having thousands of them. Or perhaps you'll be content to

grow just a few and buy dried saffron from the market. Once you've harvested and dried all the tiny orange stigmas from the center of the crocus, you'll understand the high price you have to pay.

Saffron crocus grows from a 1-inch bulbous corm. Stems are from 3 to 4 inches tall topped with a starlike lavender flower. The grasslike leaves appearing with the flower can reach 18 inches and stay green on into spring.

Plant bulbs late in summer in full sun (although they'll tolerate a bit of shade) in a rich well-drained soil. The corms multiply naturally underground. You can divide every few years.

Sage
(Salvia species)

The familiar garden sage is a hardy perennial which grows to 2 feet. It has long oval, grey-green leaves that are coarsely textured. Violet-blue flowers appear on tall spikes. A dwarf variety looks the same except is miniature.

Golden sage (*Salvia officinalis* 'Aurea') is characterized by the yellow markings on the leaf edges. It grows as easily as the common variety.

Pineapple sage (*S. elegans*) is less hardy than *S. officinalis.* It grows to a height of 2 to 3 feet. Light green leaves are delightfully fruity in fragrance. Scarlet blooms come in fall. Requirements are same as other sages.

The white and purple-red markings on the leaves make variegated sage (*S.o. var.* 'Tricolor') showier than its common parent and desirable in many landscapes.

Sage needs full sun and

grows best in poor, well-drained, somewhat dry soil. Propagate by seed, stem cuttings or layering.

Santolina
(Santolina species)

Almost indispensable to the gray garden, lavender cotton (*S. chamaecyparissus*) spreads gracefully. The narrow finely-divided leaves are whitish gray. Small round yellow flowers appear in summer. The faster growing species *S. virens* has dark green leaves and flowers in chartreuse.

Grow in full sun and any well-drained soil mixture. Keep fairly dry. Propagate by stem cuttings or layering.

Savory
(Satureja species)

Perennial or winter savory (*S. montana*), produces weak stems to 15 inches and will stand temperatures down to 10° F (–12° C). Annual summer savory grows a little larger. It is more delicately flavored than the winter variety. Small narrow leaves grow in pairs along stems. Flowers are small, pinkish white.

Both savories need full sun and well-drained soil. Annual (summer) savory prefers slightly rich soil, while the perennial (winter) species needs a sandy mix. Propagate annual savory from seed or cuttings and perennial savory by divisions, layering or root cuttings.

Sesame
(Sesamum indicum)

This tropical annual is grown for its nutty-tasting seeds. The plant grows to a height of 1 or 2 feet and has green leaves 3 to 5 inches long. There are 1-inch trumpet flowers in summer, white with pastel markings.

It's sometimes known as benne or benni.

Seed pods form inside the faded flowers and burst open to scatter the seeds. You'll need to plant a lot if you expect a quantity of seed as each plant can be harvested only once and produces about a tablespoon of seed.

Plant in full sun in any well-drained soil. It needs 120 days of hot weather and routine garden care.

Shisho
(Perilla frutescens 'Crispa')
Giving off a cinnamonlike fragrance, the 3-to 6-inch leaves of this Japanese culinary herb are dark and covered with whitish hairs on top and purple hairs underneath. The annual grows 2 to 4 feet tall and produces small pinkish flower spikes.

Plant shisho, also known as purple perilla (because of its burgundy stem) or summer coleus, in full sun or partial shade. Routine watering is sufficient. Keep the plant bushy and fuller by pinching the flower spikes as soon as they appear.

Sorrel
(Rumex species)

In this small family of the perennials, French sorrel *(R. acetosa)* has broad leaves and grows to about 2 feet; garden or French sorrel *(R. scutatus)* leaves are narrower, darker and grow about a foot taller. The flowering shoots, or dock, of French sorrel are popular in dried bouquets.

Grow in full sun and fairly moist, rich soil. Propagate from seed or root divisions.

Speedwell
(Veronica officinalis)
Popular as a ground cover, speedwell or St. Paul's betony is a perennial with creeping hairy stems and small oval, toothed leaves. Pale blue flower stalks grow from leaf junctions.

Plant speedwell in full sun or partial shade and any well-drained soil that remains fairly dry. It is difficult, if not impossible, to grow in southern coastal regions. Propagate from seed, stem cuttings, or root divisions.

Sweet Cicely
(Myrrhis odorata)
All parts of this very old herb smell and taste like anise. It's a perennial that grows 2 to 3 feet in height with fernlike foliage that's downy on the underside. The hollow stems bear small clusters of tiny white flowers in late spring, followed by shiny black seed.

Plant sweet cicely in partial shade in acid soil. Keep it moist. The edible taproot grows deep, so the bed should be prepared to accommodate. If you leave a few seeds, the plant will self-seed. Or propagate from cuttings of the taproot containing eyes.

The plant is easy to grow everywhere except in areas with warm winters. It requires cold weather.

Sweet Olive
(Osmanthus fragrans)
If you want to make potpourri or create your own fragrances, you'll certainly want to add this evergreen shrub to the garden. In home gardens it can reach a height of about 10 feet. As a container-grown plant it stays much smaller, under 3 feet indoors. Tiny white flowers in late winter and spring are highly fragrant and reminiscent of old New Orleans where it grows profusely. Leaves are finely toothed and glossy green.

Grows best in partial shade where it can be protected from the wind. Put in bright indirect light indoors. Almost any well-drained soil will do as long as it stays slightly moist.

Tansy
(Tanacetum vulgare)
The bright green leaves of this perennial are large and fernlike. Grows to 3 feet tall. Flat terminal clusters of buttonlike yellow flowers bloom late in the summer. Shorter variety *(T. v.* var. *crispum)*

is more delicate in looks. Thin clumps annually.

Tansy requires full sun, but isn't particular about soil quality. Propagate from seed or divisions.

Tarragon
(Artemisia dracunculus)

French tarragon is a perennial that spreads by rhizomes. It has slender dark green leaves. Greenish flowers bloom in small clusters. It does not bear seed.

Grow in full sun or partial shade and well-drained soil. Propagate by division or root cuttings.

Thyme
(Thymus species)
All the thymes have woody twiglike stems with tiny oval leaves. Common thyme *(T. vulgaris)* is a perennial that bushes up to 12 inches tall. A number of the creeping or wild thymes *(T. serpyl-*

lum) are more delicate in appearance.

Lemon thyme *(T. x citriodorus)* looks a lot like other thymes but the strong lemon scent distinguishes it. One variety has yellow edged leaves in keeping with the lemon theme.

Silver Thyme *(T. x c. var. 'Argentus')* is a small-leafed variety that gets its common name from its silver variegation.

All thymes require full sun and light soil that drains well. Keep thymes well clipped so they won't become woody. Propagate by divisions, stem or root cuttings.

Vanilla
(Vanilla planifolia)
Grown mostly in Mexico, this vine-like climbing orchid is valued for the seed pod or bean, the source of vanilla. Chances are your plant won't give any beans to flavor your homemade ice cream but it's ornamental to the warm greenhouse.

The rampant vine has 9-inch leaves along the fleshy stems. One variety is variegated. After the plant gets quite large it produces 3-inch greenish to yellowish flowers. Artificial pollination is necessary to produce the beanlike pods.

Provide the vanilla orchid with supports on which to climb. Pot in osmunda fiber or rich humus orchid compost. The plant thrives with lots of water and high humidity and needs shade. Propagate by seed or cuttings.

Violet, Sweet
(Viola odorata)
The deliciously sweet scent of violets is important to connoisseurs of herbal fragrances. The perennial spreads from creeping roots and forms an attrac-

tive ground cover of heart shaped leaves with crinkled edges. Flowers in deep violet, pink or white appear in late spring.

Violets are native to wooded areas and should be planted in partial shade and fairly rich soil that is kept evenly moist. Propagate from rooted offshoots or root division.

Woodruff, Sweet
(Galium odoratum)

The fragrance of sweet woodruff isn't noticeable until the leaves are dried and crushed. It's a perennial that never grows more than 14 inches high. Leaves are dark green and pointed, grow in whorls around stems. Produces profusions of tiny starlike summer flowers. Plants cannot stand drought.

Woodruff is one of the few herbs that grows well in full shade, but can take partial sun. Grow in moist, rich soil. Propagate by root divisions.

Yarrow
(Achillea millefolium)

Hardy yarrows produce flat-headed flowers in yellow, white or shades of red. Gray-green foliage is fern-like. Height varies from 8 inches to 5 feet. Cut plants back after first flowering for a second round of blooms in the fall.

Grow in full sun and well-drained soil. Propagate by division.

Five Herbs for Water Gardening

Not all herbs and spices thrive in the typical well-drained soil. Here are five to grow in the water garden—whether a slow stream in the back yard, a formally planted pool, sunken tub, or oversized containers, even indoors.

Lotus
(Nelumbo species)

Every part of the beautiful lotus is edible—its tuberous roots, leaves, flowers and seeds. The American lotus *(N. lutea)* has showy fragrant blooms and large (1 to 2 feet across) blue-green leaves that stand 2 feet above the water. The East Indian lotus, *N. nucifera,* is a larger species.

To grow from seed, plant in pots of rich soil and add a top layer of clean sand, which will keep the water clear when you submerge it 6 to 8 inches. Set 6 inches deeper in water when the plants begin to grow.

Papyrus
(Cyperus papyrus)

The stately papyrus was used by the Egyptians to make writing paper. This perennial grows to a height of 6 to 8 feet with many drooping grasslike leaves, a plume atop thick green stems.

Give the plant full sun or partial shade and keep its feet wet at all times. If possible grow in a container of rich soil submerged in shallow water. Bring indoors in winter but continue to keep the roots wet. Some people report indoor success with the plants grown in a can or pot submerged in large glazed cylinders of water. Propagate by seed or by detaching a leaf rosette and rooting in wet sand.

Sweet Flag
(Acorus calamus)

The lemon scented leaves and sweet smelling, creeping roots make this hardy perennial bog plant desirable to the herb gardener. Clumps of tall swordlike leaves grow 2 feet tall or more. A cylindrical flower spike studded with minute

Watercress grows profusely in a shaded pool.

greenish yellow flowers grows at an angle from the stem.

The plant will grow best along the edges of a water garden but can be raised in rich garden soil that's kept wet. In either case, it should be in full sun. Propagate by root division.

Water Chestnut
(Eleocharis dulcis)

You don't even need a "water garden" to grow this attractive aquatic rush plant; just a large tub of water will do.

Fill a container halfway with any ordinary topsoil and mix in a tablespoon of granular slow-release fertilizer. Add topsoil to within about 3 inches of the top and plant the water chestnut corms ½ inch below the soil surface. Submerge the pot in a container of water or a shallow pool so that its soil surface stays from ½ to 2 inches below the surface of the water. When the foliage dies down, tap the entire plant out of the pot. Wash the soil from the root mass

with a hose and gather the small brown chestnuts. (Corms are available from suppliers of aquatic plants.)

Watercress
(Nasturtium officinale)

A gourmet's delight, this creeping perennial will grow submerged, floating, or in shallow moving water. Its stems with many branches reach 2 feet or more. Dark green leaves are composed of 3 to 11 leaflets. In early summer there are clusters of small white blooms at extreme stem ends.

The peppery tasting herb grows wild in streams throughout the United States. To adapt it to home gardening, set plants or scatter seed on the edge of a moving stream or an irrigation ditch. That's all there is to it. It grows easily. In lieu of a stream, you can grow watercress in a very rich, very moist garden soil. It won't be as active but will grow. Propagate from seed or stem cuttings, even those you purchase from the greengrocer.

APPLE MINT

LAVENDER

SPEARMINT

COMMON THYME

COSTMARY

LEMON THYME

TANSY

VARIEGATED SAGE

YARROW

GOLDEN SAGE

HYSSOP

GARDEN SAGE

SILVER THYME

SOUTHERNWOOD

PENNYROYAL

DITTANY OF CRETE

CARAWAY

CATNIP

Creative Ways with Herbs and Spices

Enjoy ancient and new methods of using leaves, blooms, seeds, stems, berries or roots. Create your own fragrances, delicious foods, cosmetics, natural dyes and crafts.

Throughout history people have found innumerable ways to benefit from herbs and spices. In various forms they've been used as medicines, decoctions, salves, balms and ointments to treat every known physical and mental problem. They've been prescribed to induce sleep, to cast enchanted spells, to drive away serpents and vampires.

Herbs have made their way as symbols of victory and have played enormous roles in trade and exploration. They've been used as silent expressions of sentiment.

Leaves, flowers, roots and seeds have gone into hair colors, dyes, toothpastes, cosmetics, perfumes, air fresheners and insect repellents. People have valued them as tobacco, tea and coffee substitutes, as well as flavoring for liquors and other beverages, to say nothing of the foods of every nation.

A lot of people now grow or buy herbs for the reported healing or soothing properties. Many volumes have been written on the subject of herbal medications and home remedies. Herbalists list plants for almost any ailment.

However, in this book we're dealing only with appearance, aroma and flavor of herbs and spices. We'll explore how you can use them in cooking, creating fragrances and making cosmetics, crafts and decorations.

Herbs and spices can be blended into unique heady fragrances (opposite) or your own delicious teas (above right). They're a delight to the eyes as well as stimulating the other senses.

When it comes to self-diagnosis and self-prescription there can be genuine dangers in herbal remedies, especially to the novice. In the past herbs that are ineffectual or outright poisonous have been used as treatments for everything from snakebite to cancer. We must avoid such cruel errors and therefore here we discuss herbal medicine only in its historical context.

Nothing in this book is intended to be diagnostic or prescriptive. We assume no responsibility for the uses any reader might make of any herb or spice. The omission of poisonous herbs and spices was a deliberate decision. More ordinary herbs, however, can cause allergic reactions in some individuals. Should this happen to you, consult a physician.

Culinary Herbs and Spices

No doubt the use of herbs and spices in cooking claims the attention of more people than any of the other ways these special plants are used. In the past decade good cooks everywhere have become acquainted with seasonings known only to great chefs before. We're still rediscovering many of the wonderful flavors used for generations prior to 20th century convenience.

Herbs and spices should be used to accent and enhance the flavors of foods, not to mask and overwhelm other ingredients. Perhaps a word of caution is in order to cooks just discovering the world of spices. Practice a little restraint; don't overseason. Not every dish needs herbs or spices. But how bland many dishes would be without seasonings. Can you imagine salads, soups, sauces, stews without herbs and spices? These essential seasonings can raise the simplest foods to gourmet status. A few minced herbs added to canned soups lets the busy cook appear to be a genius at serving time.

Learn to be creative with your herbs and spices. Experiment to find flavors and quantities you enjoy. Begin with small amounts and increase as necessary. The degree of seasoning is a matter of personal preference. As you read through many of our suggestions that follow you'll note instances where no specific measurement for herbs and spices is given. It's up to you and the tastebuds of the people for whom you cook. Take our ideas as a starting point for exciting culinary adventures.

Whatever you do, don't be monotonous and repeat the same seasonings over and over. You have spices from all over the world to enjoy. Sometimes a simple change in the seasonings creates an entirely new dish.

Most complete cookbooks have tables, charts, or guides for using herbs and spices with various foods, from appetizers to desserts. Use these guidelines as handy references for basic ideas, but again, don't limit your creativity to another cook's suggestions. Of course, some home gardeners will have access to herbs that aren't included on anyone's charts.

Kitchen Equipment

The well-equipped kitchen should have a mortar and pestle for grinding and blending herbs and seeds. These utilitarian tools are made of wood, ceramic, stone, or metal. Most cooks favor wood, but the choice is really a matter of personal taste.

Keep a sharp knife and a pair of kitchen scissors handy for mincing fresh herbs or chop them on a wooden board.

Other items you'll want to have on hand include a nutmeg grater with a storage top for unused portions of the whole nutmegs, mills for grinding white and black peppercorns, other grinding mills for whole spices such as allspice and cloves and herb seeds, a press for garlic, perhaps a special grinder for sesame seeds (available from oriental food markets) and cheese-cloth and string, or a fine wire mesh tea ball for making *bouquets garnis*. If you grind a lot of herbs or spices it may be worth investing in an electric coffee grinder.

Of course, you can get along without any of these items, but herbs and spices deserve the right equipment.

Using Fresh Herbs

Gather herbs from the garden as you need them. Wash quickly in cold water when you bring them in and discard any bad leaves. Keep garden or produce-market herbs crisper for several days by storing them in sealed plastic bags or containers in the refrigerator.

Mince or chop small amounts when you need them. Flavors are quickly lost as volatile oils are released by heat. Add herbs to hot dishes at the last minute, unless it's a simmering stock.

If a recipe calls for cooking herbs in oil or butter and then browning meat in the same pan, reverse the order. Brown the meat, then add the fresh herbs. Otherwise the delicate leaves will be fried crisp, brown and undistinguishable.

Fresh Herbs on the Table

The creative cook knows that there are more herbs besides parsley to use for garnishes. Look for color among your herb varieties: sprigs of purple basil, shisho, lemon thyme, tricolor sage. Add a garland of rosemary in bloom around a crown roast. Or make a wreath of watercress accented with brightly colored nasturtiums. Gather large mature herb leaves that will cover a serving platter. Mince leaves and petals and sprinkle over vegetables. A word of warning: don't over-decorate. A couple of well-placed touches will add interest and not overwhelm the foods or the diners.

Edible Flowers

Perhaps you can't eat the daisies, but there are quite a few other blooms from the garden that have numerous culinary uses. When you gather flowers for eating, choose perfect, blemish-free specimens that have not been sprayed with any chemicals. Wash them quickly in cool water to remove dust and cut away the green stems to the base of the flower. Chill flowers in the refrigerator in a bowl of water or in a plastic bag to keep them fresh and crisp. Add to dishes at the last minute. Use sparingly to make them seem quite special.

Choose whole flowers or mince petals to garnish canapes, toss in salads, float on drinks, sprinkle on soups, cook in eggs, finish off vegetable dishes, contrast with browned meats and brighten desserts.

Among the flowers you can pick to eat are borage, calendulas, carnations and pinks, chives and onions, chrysanthemums, dandelions, fennel, geraniums, nasturtiums, rosemary, roses, salad burnet and violets. Calendulas, like safflower petals, are good substitutes for saffron.

Remember Fingerbowls?

When you serve sticky finger-foods or messy shellfish, don't forget the old-fashioned fingerbowl. To a little bowl of cool water add a bit of lemon juice and leaves of scented geraniums, lemon verbena, one of the mints, or other sweet herbs or flowers.

A Tabletop Herb Garden

In parts of the Middle East it is customary to pass a bowl of fresh herb sprigs to eat along with the meal. For a pretty, edible bouquet, just collect whatever is available from your garden or market—parsley, watercress, chives, cress, dill, cilantro, green onions, tarragon, mint—wash and chill. Arrange the sprigs in a bowl or basket. Include a few edible flowers such as borage, nasturtium, or violets, if in bloom. As a variation on the traditional idea, you could serve a spicy dip made from a yogurt base, or add the herbs to a light vinegar and oil dressing.

In Italy sprigs of fresh basil are served in little vases or vials of water on the table. Serving it in water keeps the herb from darkening or wilting.

Start your own tradition by placing a garden of herbs on the table. Give each guest a small pair of scissors along with their tableware and let them clip sprigs of fresh herbs to add to salads, soups, or other dishes.

Your tabletop garden may be just a pot of chives or several containers of assorted culinary plants. Wash the leaves under running water a couple of hours before dining and allow to drain before putting the garden on the table. Arrange the potted herbs on a wicker tray, or large dish. You may wish to construct or purchase a wooden flat or shallow tray that holds small pots or nursery flats of herbs. With a slightly deeper tray you can plant a garden right inside to carry from window to table.

Bouquets Garnis

Bouquet garni or *fagot* is a combination of several herbs, usually bay, thyme and parsley or chervil simmered in dishes as they cook. Fresh herb sprigs are simply tied with string and dropped into the cooking pot. Leaves or dried herbs are wrapped inside a 4-inch square of cheesecloth to form a bag and tied with string. You might use a fine wire mesh tea ball.

Here's a classic *bouquet garni* for soup, fish, or meat stocks:

Fresh:
2 sprigs thyme
5-6 sprigs parsley
1 bay leaf

Dried:
1 bay leaf
1 tablespoon each
   tarragon and parsley
1 teaspoon each
   rosemary and thyme

Many recipes call for a special *bouquet garni,* such as the spicy crab and shrimp boil that's unique to Louisiana. A favorite New Orleans combination goes like this:

Louisiana Bouquet Garni
1 teaspoon each whole allspice, thyme, celery seed, and black peppercorns
½ teaspoon each cayenne and whole cloves
5 bay leaves, broken
3 dried hot chile peppers

Bring about 4 quarts water to a boil and add the seasoning bag along with salt and sliced lemons. Boil for about 10 minutes before adding shellfish.

Using Preserved Herbs

To use dried herbs you'll need to break them up finely to release their stored flavor. You can simply pulverize them between your fingers as you add them to a dish or use a mortar and pestle to grind them as finely as you wish.

Since oils become concentrated in the drying process, you'll find that it usually takes less of the dried product in a recipe than it does of the fresh herb. However, the strength of the dried herb depends on how it was harvested and preserved, how it has been stored and how long you've had it on the shelves.

The old rule of thumb is:
¼ teaspoon dried, finely powdered herb = ¾ to 1 teaspoon dried, loosely crumbled herb = 1½ to 2 teaspoons fresh chopped herb.

Other equivalents to keep in mind:
½ teaspoon garlic salt = 1 clove fresh garlic (reduce other salt in recipe to compensate);
1 teaspoon dried dill seed = 1 head fresh dill;
1 tablespoon dried onion flakes = 1 medium-sized raw onion.

When you use salt-cured herbs, remove the amount of leaves you'll need and rinse away the salt just before adding them to any recipe.

To use frozen herbs, remove only the amount you'll be using. Add frozen to foods to be cooked; let herbs thaw before adding to cold foods.

If you've preserved herbs in vinegar, remove the desired amount, rinse, chop and add to recipe.

Combining Herbs

Herbs are usually used in combination. When you blend your own it's a good idea to remember that strongly flavored herbs such as marjoram, rosemary, sage and tarragon are best used alone or in combination with several milder herbs whose flavors blend easily. In most instances avoid the conflict of two strongly flavored herbs that compete for attention.

The classic herb mix of French haute cuisine is known as *fines herbes.* This is a delicate combination of three or four herbs, preferably fresh, used to flavor many dishes. The usual portions are equal parts parsley, chervil, chives and tarragon. Other mild herbs may be substituted or added.

Stoveside Herbs
The creative cook will want to have herbs and spices within arm's reach for inspired last minute additions to foods under preparation.

Keep a small pottery or porcelain pot near the stove. Add whatever sprigs or leaves are left over from daily herb harvests and uses. Reach into the herb pot for a pinch to add as you cook. The flavor will never remain constant as the herb mixture varies from day to day.

You'll probably enjoy hanging

small bunches of drying herbs near the stove to pick as needed. Use them within a couple of months as the flavor is rapidly lost when exposed to air and heat. Festive strands of dried peppers, garlic and onions last longer than herbs.

Perhaps you'd enjoy a collection of potholders stuffed with dried rosemary or other herbs. When they touch a warm dish or pan the fragrance is released in the kitchen. There are fabric prints of botanical herbs, or use any cloth that matches your kitchen. Don't forget herbed potholders when you want to give a special gift.

Mix Your Own Blend

When you find some extra time it's a good idea to prepare several premixed seasonings that you use often. This means you won't have to take the time to stir and blend each time you're in need of something special.

Stuffing Spices

All good cooks know the value of herbs and spices to stuffings and dressings for pork, poultry or veal. If you make stuffings often, try creating your own stuffing spice mix. Among the dried herbs that are excellent stuffing additions are sage, parsley, rosemary, marjoram, thyme, nutmeg, fennel and oregano. Add other favorites and blend them to suit your tastebuds.

Seasoned Flour

Keep a jar of flour well-seasoned with herbs and spices to add to gravies and sauces, biscuits or pizza crusts, or to dust foods before frying.

Simply add 1 to 2 teaspoons mixed dried herbs and spices to 2 cups flour. Add ½ teaspoon salt and freshly ground black pepper to taste. Seal tightly.

Spice Parisienne

Also known as *quatre spices,* this is a classic mixture of spices used to enhance desserts and meats.
1 tablespoon ground cinnamon
1 teaspoon each ground cloves, ginger and nutmeg

Pickling Spice

When the pickling season approaches you might take the time to prepare a quantity of pickling spices that are called for in many recipes. Prepare your own blend of herbs and spices by mixing various portions, according to taste, of whole allspice, bay leaves, black peppercorns, cardamom, cinnamon sticks, cloves, coriander seed, dill seed, mustard seed, red peppers, ground ginger and mace.

Chili Powders

The commercial "spice" sold as chili powder is a mixture based on several types of sweet peppers (paprika) and hot peppers such as cayenne. Ingredients such as cumin, cloves, coriander, oregano, turmeric, black pepper or garlic may be added. Pungency ranges from mild to fiery hot according to the amount of hot peppers used.

To blend your own chili seasoning start with several tablespoons of paprika and add other spices according to taste. Mix small quantities to use as needed for Mexican and Spanish dishes or blend a larger portion of the spices together and store in an airtight jar. Use whenever you feel inspired to add a touch of chili flavor to eggs, rice, gravies, sauces, soups, fish, meats and vegetables.

Keep both fresh and preserved herbs and spices within easy reach when you are cooking. Herb-filled pot holders add tempting fragrances.

Curry Powders

Curry seasonings are at their best when the spices are freshly ground and mixed together at the last minute. The busy cook, however, may want to blend enough favorite spices at one time to store in a tightly closed jar for instant spicing. In pretty jars or tins curry powder is a good gift, too. Your own creation will no doubt be better suited to your way of cooking than the commercial powders. Try this typical blend for starters.

- 4 tablespoons each *coriander and fenugreek seeds*
- 1 teaspoon each *mustard and fennel seeds*
- 2 tablespoons each *cardamom seed, white peppercorns and ground ginger*
- 3 tablespoons *ground turmeric*
- 1 tablespoon *cayenne or red chili (for hot curry) or ½ tablespoon pepper (for milder curry)*

Powder ingredients together with a mortar and pestle, blender or food processor.

Tangy Condiments

Herbs and spices are right at home when added to mustards, relishes and salts. Try these suggestions for starters.

Herbed Salt

A survey of the supermarket spice shelves will reveal a number of herbed salts. Prepare your own flavored salts for salad greens, fresh raw vegetables and many cooked dishes. Reduce the amount of regular salt in the recipe when adding a bit of herbed salt, or use in place of the suggested amount. Use only one kind of herb or blend combinations that please your taste. Dried lemon peel blends nicely with many herbs if you'd like a salt that has a touch of lemon flavor.

Spread a thin layer of plain (noniodized) table salt on a baking sheet. Cover with a layer of fresh chopped herbs. Top with another layer of salt. Place in a medium oven for about 10 minutes. Break up lumps that result from leaf moisture and return to the oven for another 10 minutes or until leaves crumble easily.

Thoroughly blend the salt and herbs in a mortar and pestle or blender. Add ground pepper or paprika and dried ground spices, if desired. Store in tightly capped jars. Don't forget labels.

Making Mustards

Everyone has a favorite taste in mustard and indeed there is great variety in flavors that can be created according to how you mix it. Once you've found the flavor you enjoy, you'll never be happy with ready-made mustard again.

Mustard making is easy. It's best to mix in small quantities because although mustard keeps indefinitely, the flavor changes very rapidly.

To prepare hot mustard use a cold liquid at the ratio of 2 or 3 tablespoons liquid to ¼ cup dry mustard powder.

For an English style mustard, vinegar is the liquid. For a spicier taste, use white wine. For the French Dijon flavor, add champagne to the powder.

Flat beer turns the mustard powder into the spicy Chinese variety. For the hottest of all, use plain water as the liquid.

To tone down the mustard, thin with a little milk, mayonnaise, or olive oil. Vary mustard flavor by adding sugar, pressed garlic, tarragon or other spices to the powdered mustard before adding the liquid.

When the mustard is well-blended, pour into a container and top with a lemon slice to help retain freshness. Replace the lemon weekly. Seal with a tightfitting cap. Store in the refrigerator.

For a mild mustard enjoyed by many people on American hot dogs and burgers try the following method. Place ½ cup dry mustard in a heatproof dish. Add just enough boiling water to make a paste. Then cover the paste with boiling water to completely im-

Making your own curry powders *(left)* and mustards *(opposite)* allows you control of the degree of hotness and insures freshness. Packed into interesting containers both make spicy gifts.

merse it. Allow to stand for about 20 to 30 minutes, or until steaming stops. As it cools, churn the mustard away from the sides with a rubber spatula. Allow to settle for a few minutes and drain off the water.

Cover again with boiling water. Let stand for 5 minutes and drain again. Add 4 teaspoons sugar and 1 teaspoon salt, or to taste. If you wish, add a little vinegar or other spices. For a bright yellow color, add 1 teaspoon turmeric. Pour into a container and allow to cool completely. Seal tightly and store at room temperature.

French Herb Mustard

¼ cup dry mustard
¼ cup white wine vinegar
⅓ cup dry white wine
¼ cup brown sugar
½ teaspoon salt
½ teaspoon each *dill seed, whole cloves, and whole allspice*
3 egg yolks

Yield: 1 cup.

Mix together all ingredients except the egg yolks and allow to stand 2 hours. Whisk yolks into mixture. Transfer mixture to the top of a double boiler. Cook, stirring constantly, over hot, not boiling, water, until mustard thickens (about 5 minutes). Cool mustard. Cover and refrigerate up to 1 month.

Nasturtium Capers

If you don't grow real capers you can make a pretty good substitute from the green buds of nasturtiums.

Cover buds with a brine composed of 1 cup salt to 2 quarts water. Weight the buds down with a heavy plate to keep them immersed for 24 hours. Then remove the buds and soak in cold water for 1 hour. Drain.

Bring distilled white vinegar to a boil. Pack the buds into sterilized jars to within ½ inch of the top and cover with the boiling vinegar. Seal and process in a boiling water bath for 10 minutes, or store in the refrigerator; use within a few weeks.

Fresh Horseradish vs. Dried

There's no doubt about it, fresh horseradish is tastier than the dried form, which can become bitter if kept too long. Fresh roots of horseradish will keep a long time when stored in a cool place. If you don't grow your own, stock up from the produce markets when the fresh roots are available, usually in late summer and early fall. Horseradish roots also freeze successfully. After about 3 months they become bitter.

To assure full potency make small batches of horseradish frequently and do not store it more than 2 or 3 weeks.

Peel washed roots, grate or cube desired amount and put through the food processor or blender with vinegar, salt and sugar to taste. Pack in jars, cap tightly and store in refrigerator.

If you must resort to dried horseradish root powder, reconstitute it about 30 minutes before serving. Mix 1 tablespoon dried powder in 2 tablespoons water and add about ½ cup heavy cream. Just before serving add salt, sugar and a bit of vinegar to taste.

Serve fresh or reconstituted horseradish with cold meats, smoked fish, sausages and frankfurters. Stir into seafood cocktail sauces, potato or pasta salads, as well as French dressings. Blend with whipped cream for a quick cold buffet sauce. Add to hot cream or white sauces and serve with boiled or corned beef, London broil or prime rib.

Well-Dressed Salads

It's worth planting an herb garden if only to make salad dressings.

Herb Dressing

Use basil, dill, marjoram, oregano, sage, tarragon, thyme or other culinary favorites in this reliable oil and vinegar dressing.

6 tablespoons oil
3 tablespoons vinegar
¼ teaspoon each *salt and dry mustard*
  Freshly ground pepper to taste
1 or 2 cloves *garlic, peeled and minced or pressed*
2 or 3 tablespoons *fresh herbs, minced, or 1 tablespoon dried herbs, crushed*

Combine, shake and chill.

For fruit salads omit mustard and garlic and add sugar or honey to taste. Use poppyseed, rosemary, tarragon, or other sweet herbs.

Tabbouli Salad

This refreshing and unusual salad from the Middle East uses garden-fresh herbs as main ingredients. You may wish to add diced green peppers or avocados.

1 cup bulghur (cracked wheat)
2 cups boiling water
2 cups parsley, finely chopped
½ cup green onions, finely chopped
½ cup fresh mint, chopped, or ¼ cup dried mint, crumbled
½ cup lemon juice
½ teaspoon salt, or to taste
  Freshly grated black pepper, to taste
1 teaspoon allspice
½ cup olive oil
3 ripe tomatoes, peeled and diced
  Lettuce leaves, preferably romaine
  Lemon wedges

Pour boiling water over the bulghur in a bowl and let stand 1 hour. Drain and return to bowl. Add the parsley, onions, mint, lemon juice, salt, pepper and allspice. Blend well and chill.

Just before serving toss with oil and chopped tomatoes. Serve on lettuce and garnish with lemon.

Whether gathered from the home garden or the greengrocer, garlic, leeks, scallions, peppers, chives, parsley and other fresh herbs add new dimensions to salads as major ingredients or seasonings.

Build Up a Cellar of Flavored Vinegars

One of the most pleasurable things you can do with herbs and spices is to create flavored vinegars. Colorful and varied vinegars in interesting bottles are not only visual assets to the kitchen shelves, but nice to have on hand when you want to perk up a salad dressing or add zest to dishes calling for vinegar. It's like having a good choice of wines to call on.

You can use almost every herb and spice, alone or in combination. Experiment with small quantities of various mixes to find flavors you enjoy. Pretty bottles with a sprig of herb immersed in the vinegar make welcome gifts. Take a corked bottle of flavored vinegar instead of wine to your next dinner party. Your hosts will be delighted.

The flavoring procedure is simple. Just add 4 ounces fresh herb or spice, or 2 ounces of the dried version to each quart of cold vinegar. Leave for five to six weeks to develop flavor. Then strain the vinegar into clean bottles, or leave fresh herb twigs in for show. Cap tightly and store. (You can seal with hot wax to which pungent powdered cinnamon has been added.) Your palate will let you know if you need to add more or less next time.

As the base you can use any of several store-bought vinegars—white, wine, cider, or malt. The white vinegar will let the flavor of the herb or spice shine through. Other vinegars add their own characteristics to the end product.

If you want flavored vinegar in a hurry, bring the vinegar and spices to a boil and simmer for about 20 minutes. Pour into bottles and cap. It's ready to use without waiting for it to mellow.

Butters, Cheeses and Sauces

The following ideas blend garden fresh or dried seasonings in spreads, dips or smooth sauces. Experiment with variations.

Herbed Butters

Flavored butter adds a special touch to hot breads, baked potatoes and vegetables. It's a tasty sandwich spread and makes an event of a stack of toast. Use it to cook eggs or toss noodles and other pasta. Melt it on broiled meats and fish.

Any of your favorite herbs will make delicious butter. Don't forget to try some with flower petals, too. Use 1 tablespoon fresh minced herb or 1 teaspoon dried herb or crushed seed to each ¼ cup softened butter, sweet or salted as you prefer. Mix well and pack into small dishes or form into butter balls. Refrigerate overnight to develop flavor fully.

If you want to go all the way you might pass a variety of herbed butters at a special meal. Identify each flavor with a garnish of the fresh herb.

Herbed Cheese and Mayonnaise

Transform cottage cheese or cream cheese into dips and spreads by adding herbs and spices. To 8 ounces of softened cream cheese or ½ pound of cottage cheese add 2 tablespoons minced fresh herbs or 1 teaspoon dried herbs or spices. Combine compatible flavors as desired. Add a bit of pepper sauce if you like it hot. If you want a smoother or thinner product add sour cream, yogurt, or mayonnaise. Make several hours or a day ahead and leave in the refrigerator to develop the flavors.

A well-seasoned cheeseball is nice for a party or a gift. Start with feta goat cheese or good sharp grated cheddar. Combine with butter, herbs and spices according to taste. Form into balls with your hands. To make the cheese festive, roll in finely chopped nuts, finely minced fresh herbs, or crushed seeds. Wrap in cheesecloth, foil or waxed paper and refrigerate for at least a full day. Bring to room temperature about an hour before serving. Garnish with fresh herbs.

Seasoned mayonnaise can serve as a dip for raw vegetables, a sandwich spread, or a dressing for cold seafood or mixed vegetable salads.

Make your favorite blender-style mayonnaise or use a bottled product. Stir in minced fresh herbs, a bit of lemon peel and whatever spices you enjoy. Mix well; chill.

Korozott Liptoi

1 cup cottage cheese, sieved
1 cup butter or margarine, softened
1 tablespoon caraway seeds
1 tablespoon each minced capers and chives
1 tablespoon dry mustard
1 chopped anchovy (optional)
Paprika

Combine all ingredients and beat smooth. Dust with paprika. Makes 2 cups.

Pesto Sauce

One of the great Italian contributions to the world of foods is this sauce made from fresh basil. It's usually served on pasta that's been cooked *al dente*. Try a dollop in vegetable soups, on baked potatoes, broiled fish or golden spaghetti squash.

2 cups firmly packed fresh basil leaves, washed and drained
¼ cup pignoli (pine nuts), walnuts or pistachios
3 cloves garlic, peeled
¾ cup freshly grated Parmesan cheese
½ cup olive oil

Blend basil, nuts and garlic until pureed. Blend in cheese. Slowly add oil while blending on low speed. Serve immediately or add a thin layer of olive oil, cover and refrigerate. The oil keeps the sauce from darkening until serving time. If making a lot for later, divide into small portions and freeze.

Pesto sauce of crushed fresh basil leaves is an Italian classic served over pasta.

During basil season make plenty of pesto and freeze small quantities of it in individual containers or plastic bags. Thaw for 2 hours before serving or place in a bowl of hot water for about 20 minutes before opening.

Do not attempt pesto with dried basil. But you can use fresh parsley if necessary. The taste is different, of course, but good.

Herbed Pasta

In lieu of pesto, here's another easy sauce that's delicious on hot spaghetti or other pasta.

Mince ½ cup fresh herbs such as chives, basil, parsley, thyme, savory, oregano, or whatever is in the garden. Mix the herbs with ½ cup softened butter. Quickly sauté several cloves of crushed garlic in ½ cup olive oil and add the butter mixture to melt. Pour over pasta and toss. Pass freshly grated Romano or Parmesan cheese.

Basting Sauce and Marinade for Meats

To impart the flavors of herbs and spices, marinate meats prior to cooking or baste with herbed sauce as they cook.

Suggested seasonings:

Beef/bay, oregano, rosemary, savory, thyme

Lamb/coriander, basil, cumin, mint, parsley, rosemary

Pork/anise, caraway, cumin, nutmeg, parsley, rosemary, thyme

Poultry/basil, parsley, rosemary, tarragon

For basting: To each cup of meat stock, add ½ cup wine and 2 tablespoons fresh herbs or 1 tablespoon dried. Simmer together for 10 minutes. Baste meat several times.

For marinade: Combine 1 cup oil, ½ cup wine or vinegar, salt and pepper to taste, 1 clove crushed garlic and herbs and spices to taste. Pour over meat and cover several hours before cooking.

Add New Flavors to Baking

The wonderful aroma of herbed bread baking in the oven doubles the delight.

To your basic bread or biscuit dough add about 2 tablespoons, minced, fresh chives, dill, marjoram, sage, savory, or thyme. Or you can use 2 teaspoons of any of these herbs dried. Try mixing several herbs and ground spices.

Seeds of caraway, dill, fennel, anise, sesame and the familiar poppy make interesting and tasty toppings on breads, rolls, biscuits and cookies. Just brush the dough with egg yolk and sprinkle with seeds before baking.

Seeds can be used in less familiar ways. Add fennel to apple and berry pies, cobblers or tarts. Crushed coriander gives a new dimension to hot gingerbread. To vary your basic cookie dough or cake batter, add crushed coriander, anise, dill, sesame, or fennel before baking. Stir in a few toasted sesame seeds next time you make a pie crust. Create a new dessert by substituting toasted sesame seeds for the pecans in your favorite pecan pie recipe. Add a half cup of raisins for tart contrast.

Herb Pastry Mix for Quiche

For each 9-inch pastry shell combine 1½ cups flour, 1 tablespoon dried parsley flakes, 2 teaspoons dill weed, 1½ teaspoons dry mustard and ¼ teaspoon salt. You can blend enough for several crusts and store in tightly covered jar.

When you're ready for a crust, cut ½ cup butter or margarine into 1½ cups of this pastry mix until it resembles coarse meal. Sprinkle in 4 to 5 tablespoons cold water, a tablespoon at a time, until the mix is moist enough to leave sides of bowl. Gather into ball. Roll out on floured surface to ⅛ inch thick. Line quiche pan or pie plate. Prick with fork, brush with beaten egg and bake at 400° F (204° C) for 10 minutes. Prepare any quiche filling, pour it into the partially baked shell and finish the baking according to your recipe.

Herbs and spices impart new tastes, aromas and looks to breads. Blend into dough or sprinkle seed over top before baking.

Sugar and Spice

Edible parts of herbs and spices can be turned into treats to satisfy the sweet tooth.

Crystallized Leaves and Petals

Sugar-coated herb petals and leaves can be used as garnishes for desserts or eaten as candy. Pick roses, violets, johnny-jump-ups, or attractive leaves of borage, sage, mint or other sweet foliage.

Wash the petals or leaves quickly and gently pat dry with a paper towel. Remove individual flower petals. Cut away the bitter white tip of rose petals.

Beat egg whites until foamy and brush it on each side of the leaves or petals with a pastry brush or your fingers. Surfaces should be moist but with no excess egg white.

Shake or dust fine granulated white sugar on both sides. Place gently on a tray. Dry in the refrigerator for several days.

Candied Blossoms

Violets, borage, roses, geraniums, violas and other edible flowers are pretty finishing touches on custards, cakes, ice creams, sherbets, parfaits and other light desserts. Or simply serve them in a bowl or little basket as candy.

Start with about 3 cups of blooms. Wash quickly and remove stems. Pat dry with paper towels.

Combine 3 cups white sugar with 2 cups water, bring to boil and cook to the soft crack stage—about 238° F (114° C) on a candy thermometer. Pour about half the syrup into a shallow pan and let both quantities cool. Position the flowers on a rack inside the pan so they float on the syrup. Cover top of the pan with a damp cloth and let it sit in a cool place for several hours. Then cover the flowers with the remaining cooled syrup. Let stand at least 12 hours in a cool place with a cloth over the pan to keep dust out.

Remove the rack and place it where the flowers can drain and dry. When completely dried, store flowers in an airtight container between layers of waxed paper to prevent them from sticking together.

Candied Angelica Stems

The stalks of angelica or lovage can be candied and used as a fruitcake ingredient or garnish.

Harvest mature stalks and cut into pieces 3 or 4 inches long. Soak 12 hours in a solution of cold water and 1 tablespoon *each* salt and vinegar. Drain and cover with fresh water. Boil until stalks are transparent.

Make a syrup of 2 cups white sugar and 1 cup water. Add a few drops green food coloring, if desired. Place the stems in the syrup and simmer until transparent and glazed. Place on a tray until dry. Store in airtight containers in a cool place.

Horehound Candy

A generation ago this bittersweet candy was a cough suppressant. Now it's made out of nostalgia.

Boil 1 quart chopped horehound leaves and stems in a pint of water for 30 minutes to make a strong decoction. Add 3 cups white sugar and bring to a boil. Add ¼ cup butter and continue cooking until the syrup forms a hard ball in cold water—250° F (121° C) on a candy thermometer. Pour into a buttered shallow pan. Cool. When hard, cut into squares and wrap individually in waxed paper. Store in a closed container.

Spiced Sugar

To flavor granulated sugar, consider using leaves of scented geraniums, mints, sweet cicely, bee balm, or petals of roses, pinks, or violets. For spiced sugar add ground cinnamon, cloves, ginger, or allspice. Store on the spice shelves and add to puddings, toppings, meringues, syrups, cereals, waffles, crepes, beverages.

Put alternating layers of granulated white or brown sugar and leaves, petals, or spices in a wide-mouthed crock or other container. Close tightly. After a couple of weeks blend thoroughly. Store in air-tight containers.

Jellies flavored with herbs and spices make festive gifts.

Herbal Honey

Fill a pretty jar with any honey you prefer. Add a whole bay leaf, or several pieces of crystallized ginger studded with whole cloves —or several thin slices of lemon and a cinnamon stick.

Herb or Spice Jellies

Jellies made from apple or other fruit juices and herbs or spices are good with roast meats. And they make tasty gifts. Adapt the basic recipe to almost any culinary herb: basil, fennel, mint, rosemary, sage, scented geraniums, thyme. Suitable spices include allspice, cloves, cinnamon and ginger.

3 cups fruit juice (see below)
¼ to ½ cup fresh herb, chopped, or 2 tablespoons dried herb or spice seed, crushed
2 tablespoons cider vinegar
3 to 3½ cups granulated sugar
½ cup liquid pectin
Fresh herb sprigs or whole spices (optional)
Few drops food coloring (optional)

Bring 1 cup of fruit juice to a rolling boil, pour over herb or spice and let stand 20 minutes. Strain into large saucepan. Add vinegar, the remaining 2 cups of fruit juice and appropriate coloring, if desired. Mix in sugar and bring to a boil. Stir in pectin and boil 1 minute more. Remove from heat and skim off foam. Pour into hot, sterilized pint or half-pint jars. Add a sprig or few leaves of the herb or pieces of the spice on top or immerse in the jelly. Use melted paraffin wax or lids to seal.

Juice and herb combinations:

Cloves and tangerine juice
Mint and apple juice
Marjoram and orange juice
Tarragon and grape juice
Thyme and crabapple juice.

Rose Hip Jam and Jelly

No other food in the garden rivals the fruit of roses for concentrated food value. It is one of the richest sources of vitamin C and contains large amounts of other vitamins and minerals. Old species of roses, especially *Rosa rugosa*, produce the tastiest and most nutritious hips. Harvest when the hips turn bright orange-red. Remove blossom ends and stems, wash well.

To make jam: Simmer 2 cups rose hips in 2 cups water until tender, mashing the fruit while it cooks to release juices. Push the fruit through a fine sieve. Add 1 cup sugar for each cup pulp. Cook until the mixture has the consistency of jam. Pour into sterilized jars and seal with melted paraffin wax or lids.

For jelly: Soak 1 quart dried apples overnight in enough water to cover. The following morning clean 1 quart hips and combine with apples in a pan with just enough water to cover. Cook until tender. Drain through a jelly bag. Add 2 cups sugar to each pint of juice and boil about 20 minutes, or until mixture jells into a thick mass when dropped from a spoon into cold water. Pour into sterilized jars and seal.

Both the jam and jelly can be made from dried rose hips available in organic food stores.

Rose Petal Jam

Make this jam for an exotic taste treat on muffins, cakes and toast. Caution: do not use petals of roses that have been sprayed with chemicals.

1 pound fresh rose petals
2 pounds sugar
Hot water
Juice of 1 lemon

Pack layers of petals tightly in a large crock with alternating layers of sugar, finishing with a layer of sugar. Cover with hot water. Put a damp cloth over the crock and let stand for 3 days.

Then prepare a syrup, using enough water to dissolve one pound of sugar. Cook the syrup to soft ball stage, 234° to 240° F (112° to 116° C), then add the rose petals and any juice they formed. Let the mixture simmer until it reaches the consistency of honey. Remove from heat and stir in lemon juice. Pour into hot sterilized jars and seal.

Herbal Teas and Other Beverages

Classically, tea refers to the leaves of the oriental shrub *Camellia sinensis* (formerly called *Thea sinensis*). The term "tea" has come to apply to all drinks made from steeping leaves, flowers, seeds, roots or bark in hot water. In the broad sense all teas are "herbal" teas since they are made from useful plant parts. Current usage, however, classifies oriental teas separately from non-caffeine herbal teas.

Oriental tea comes in three forms: black (fermented), Oolong (semi-fermented) from India and Ceylon and green (unfermented) from China and Japan. Prices vary according to variety and quality.

To brew a perfect pot of tea start with a good quality loose tea. Warm a nonmetal teapot with hot water and drain. Put 1 teaspoon of tea in the pot for each cup, plus an extra one for the pot. Bring freshly drawn water to a boil and immediately pour over the leaves. Steep 3 to 5 minutes, stirring the leaves once to distribute flavor. Pour through a strainer into tea-cups or glasses. You may add a sweetener, lemon or milk as you prefer. Some English insist on pouring the milk into the cup before adding the hot tea to avoid scalding the milk. Of course, there are those who do it in reverse, including Queen Elizabeth.

If the tea proves too strong, add hot water. A proper tea table always has a pot of hot water handy. If you're making tea to serve over ice, add extra leaves for a stronger brew to allow for the melting ice.

To add variety, mix into any tea a few dried or fresh herb leaves, bits of lemon or orange peel, flowers, pieces of cinnamon or vanilla bean, cloves or other whole spices. Store tea leaves or mixes in tight containers, preferably tin boxes.

Even though herbal teas are growing in popularity in America, they're certainly not new. They've

Teas from the Orient come in three forms: black or fermented, Oolong or semifermented, and green or unfermented. They are joined by American and European teas made of one kind of herb or blends. Add variety to tea drinking by mixing your own herbs and spices with commercial teas.

The English popularized Oriental teas as evidenced by this old label. In recent years health food advocates have brought alternative herbal teas to an increased popularity.

been enjoyed in many countries for centuries. Herbal drinks were known in Europe long before oriental teas entered the local picture. American Indians and colonists drank herbal concoctions. The Orientals wonder why we import so much of their tea when we have sage in our gardens. New Englanders have enjoyed sage tea sweetened with a bit of maple syrup for generations. Brazil is one of the world's leading producers of coffee, yet the favorite drink there seems to be *yerba mate,* made from a member of the holly family and sipped from a carved gourd through a *bombilla* or tube. Now the rest of the world is discovering the delicious flavor of *mate.* It contains a small amount of caffeine. Another caffeine tea can be brewed from the African cola nut which is used in cola drinks.

Herbal teas may be made from just one kind of herb or a mixture of several, with flowers and spices added if you like. Elaborate blends are available commercially but try experimenting and pack your own favorite blends in tins for gift giving or to enjoy yourself.

Teas brewed from the leaves of herbs are also called tisanes. Most are made by *infusion,* that is, steeping in hot water. Start with 2 to 3 teaspoons fresh or frozen leaves or 1 to 2 teaspoons dried herb per cup in a nonmetal teapot that's been warmed. Cover with the proper amount of boiling water and steep 5 to 10 minutes. Strain into cups. Sweeteners or lemon may be added as desired. Milk is rarely used with herbal teas as it clouds the drink and disguises the subtle flavors. All herbal teas may be served iced. Just make them a little stronger to allow for the melting ice.

Some herb leaves, as well as seeds, roots and bark must be prepared by *decoction*—boiling the herb in water to draw out the flavors. Add the herb or spice to water at about the same ratio as in steeped tea. Boil for 15 to 20 minutes and strain into teacups. Add lemon and sweeteners, as desired.

Here's a decoction made from fresh ginger root that deserves special attention. It proves perfect refreshment on a cold day and is delicious iced.

Scott's Ginger Tea

Grate or chop about 2 tablespoons fresh ginger root (no need to peel) into 4 cups water. Add half a lemon, sliced. Bring to the boil and continue boiling, uncovered, for about 15 to 20 minutes. Strain into cups. Add honey to taste. For variety, add a cinnamon stick, a few cardamom seeds or whole cloves along with the fresh ginger.

Coffee and Its Substitutes

We can think of coffee as an herbal drink since it's made from the seed of a plant, *Coffea arabica.*

Buy the beans, roasted or green, whole or ground and store in refrigerator or freezer to maintain freshness longer. If you roast your own you can control richness of the brew. Grinding the roasted beans at the last minute insures a better taste, provided the beans were high quality to start with.

There are numerous coffee makers on the market. Make coffee according to directions that come with your pot or brewing equipment. If you're like most coffee lovers, you'll probably prefer the flavor made from dripping methods over those that perk or boil the brew.

To add an occasional spicy touch to dessert coffee, add a whole cardamom seed or a few crushed coriander seeds to the cup. Cinnamon and coffee are good companions, add a sprinkle before making the coffee or use a cinnamon stick to stir the brew. Top with whipped cream and sprinkle with cinnamon.

Many people cannot or prefer not to drink high-caffeine coffee. They can substitute decaffeinated beans or other herbs. New Or-leans has made the addition of chicory root to coffee famous but chicory can also be brewed alone as a coffee replacement. Other people enjoy asparagus seeds, dandelion root, English oak acorns, hawthorn seeds, Kava-Kava, milk thistle seeds, soybeans or witch grass roots. All these substitutes are roasted and ground.

Other Good Things to Drink

On a cold evening nothing beats hot mulled cider, wine or apple juice. Pour the chosen beverage into a saucepan. Combine desired spices such as cinnamon sticks, whole cloves, allspice, citrus peel, flower petals in a cheesecloth bag or wire mesh tea ball. Simmer for about 15 minutes or longer, but do not boil. Pour into cups, mugs, or glasses. Garnish with spices.

Freshly ground nutmeg is delicious in hot steamed milk (with a piece of vanilla bean), cold eggnog, or other milk-based beverages. Keep pieces of nutmeg in the top of your nutmeg grater.

For tasty cold punches, start with a base of iced herbal tea, add whatever fruit juices you like along with sparkling wine, carbonated ginger ale or soda water. Blend together. Add a ring or block of ice in which you've frozen sprigs of herbs or flowers. Garnish the bowl, pitcher, or glasses with borage leaves and flowers, any of the mints, rose petals, or violets.

Dandelion Wine

Pick dandelion flowers that have just begun to open. Harvest only those you know have not been sprayed with any chemical. Follow this old New England recipe.

2½ gallons dandelion flowers, removed from stems
6   oranges, thinly sliced
10 pounds sugar
4   gallons lukewarm water

Make 6 alternate layers of flowers, sugar and oranges in a 5-gallon crock. Pour water over and cover with a cloth. Leave at room temperature until bubbling stops, usually about 3 weeks. Strain the sweet wine into bottles through a double layer of cheesecloth. Cap bottles and store in cool, dry place.

Turn a big mugful of coffee into something special with whipped cream and spices.

Herbal Teas from Leaves
(Made by infusion, steeping in hot water)

Alfalfa	Lemon verbena
Angelica	Marjoram
Blackberry	Mate
Borage	Mint
Catnip	Oat straw
Coltsfoot	Red clover
Comfrey	Rosemary
Damiana	Sage
Dill	Savory
Dittany of Crete	Scented geraniums
Germander	Strawberry
Great mullein	Thyme
Horehound	Betony
Lemongrass	Yerba buena

Herbal Teas from Flowers
(Infusion)

Calendula	Jasmine
Chamomile	Lime
Goldenrod	Malva
Hibiscus	Rose

Herbal Teas from Leaves
(Made by decoction, boiling the herb in water)

Agrimony	Lemon balm
Bergamot	

Herbal Teas from Seeds, Roots and Bark
(Decoction)

Anise	Dandelion
Birch	Ginger
Cardamom	Ginseng
Cinnamon	Sassafras

Preserving Garden Fragrances

The fragrances of a garden bring back many memories to each of us. A certain smell takes you back to some special place, time or event, even if you aren't consciously aware of the association. As Rudyard Kipling put it, "Scents are surer than sounds or sights to make your heart strings crack."

The heady, nostalgic aromas that blend together so perfectly in the garden can be captured in potpourris and other concoctions that last indefinitely. These pleasant smells come back like summertime whenever you open a box or jar of fragrant herbs.

And even if you don't garden, it's possible to buy dried petals, leaves, spices and oils, the same ingredients that are the basis of costly perfumes, to create your own special scents at home. Herb and spice shops, as well as organic food and soap shops offer all kinds of dried leaves and petals and essential oils. Other ingredients are available at pharmacies.

Potpourris, Sachets and Tussie Mussies

Long before modern air fresheners came in cans, the leaves, flowers, seeds, roots and barks of herbs and spices were carried in hand bouquets, strewn on the floor or preserved in special blends to freshen the air or mask unwanted odors.

Floral or spicy potpourri can perfume a room or be stuffed into tiny pillows for freshening clothes

Herbal pillows

or linen. Stuff a larger pillow for pleasant afternoon napping.

Potpourris are blends of flowers, fragrant leaves and spices with a fixative added to preserve the essential oils. Orrisroot, calamus (sweet flag), benzoin, storax and ambergris are the most commonly used fixatives. All are available at drugstores or from herbalists. A few drops of fragrant oils complete the mixes.

Moist Potpourri

Potpourris in earlier times were made by the moist method where herbs are salted down in a crock, then mixed with spices, oils, a fixative and a bit of brandy or good perfume. The fragrances last for many years.

To make the old-fashioned moist version, start with petals and fragrant leaves collected from the garden. Dry them only partially, for just a few days, until they're limp but not crispy dry. Layer the petals with noniodized salt in a wide-mouthed container, adding spices, fixative, fragrant oils and brandy or alcohol-based perfume. Place a weight on top of the mixture to help draw out the oils. Cover tightly.

Open the container, remove the weight and stir the mixture every day for about a month or until the fragrances are blended and mellowed. Then pour into a large bowl and mix very thoroughly. Pack into small containers of opaque glass, porcelain or silver that have removable lids. Open the cover whenever you wish to enjoy the fragrance. If the potpourri seems to be drying out, add a little perfume or good brandy over the top and stir to activate the oils.

Half-Century Potpourri

Here's one recipe for moist potpourri you can use as a guide for creating your own. It's called the half-century potpourri because the fragrance lasts 50 years or more.

¾ cup salt (noniodized)
3 bay leaves, crushed
¼ cup allspice, crushed
¼ cup cloves, crushed
¼ cup brown sugar
1 tablespoon orrisroot powder
1 quart partially dried rose petals, preferably old species

2 cups mixed, partially dried, fragrant garden flowers (jasmine, lavender, orange blossoms, violets, etc.)
1 cup dried fragrant leaves (rose geranium, bee balm, lemon verbena, etc.)
2 tablespoons brandy

Mix together the salt, bay, allspice, cloves and sugar. Blend flower petals and leaves with orrisroot. Place some of the petal mixture in a large crock and sprinkle with the salt mixture. Continue alternating layers of petals and salt, ending with salt. Add the brandy, weight down with a plate and cap tightly. After stirring every day and mixing thoroughly at the end of a month, pour into small containers.

It's said that this old recipe will keep its fragrance for up to 50 years, with the addition of a bit of brandy every couple of years or whenever the mixture dries out.

Potpourri containers

Dry Potpourri

Dry potpourri begins with thoroughly dried, crispy petals and leaves. Then they're combined with fixatives, spices and fragrant oils, stored in a covered container for several weeks, shaken from time to time to blend. After the mellowing period, place in small containers with removable lids or stuff into little bags or pillows as sachets. A typical dry potpourri goes like this:

San Francisco Potpourri

1 quart dried flower petals
1 cup small whole flowers (dried in silica gel or borax)
2 cups dried fragrant leaves
1 tablespoon crushed orrisroot
2 tablespoons dried citrus peel
1 teaspoon anise seed, crushed

1 tablespoon each *whole cloves,*
  allspice, cardamom seed, all
  crushed
1 *whole nutmeg, crushed*
2 *bay leaves, broken*
4 *cinnamon sticks, broken*
1 *vanilla bean, broken*
  Several drops each oils of
  patchouli, jasmine, rose
  geranium, lilac and tuberose

Place petals, blooms and leaves in
a large container, packing loosely
so there's plenty of room to shake
the mixture. Sprinkle with orrisroot.
Add the citrus peel and spices
and mix together gently. Sprinkle
the oils on top and close tightly.
Shake the container every few
days for about six weeks or until
the mixture is well mellowed. Then
pack into smaller containers, sachets or gift packages.

It's always difficult to predict the
exact fragrance you'll end up with
when you make potpourri. A lot
depends upon the condition, variety and freshness of the flowers
and foliages you start with as well
as how they're dried. Refer to our
list of fragrance garden plants
(page 17) for suggested herbs to
include in potpourri. Take a walk
through your entire garden and
look for any flowers and leaves
that smell good. Also, collect a few
flowers that have nice color even
if they don't have fragrance. They'll
add a lot to the visual quality of a
dry potpourri.

Collect ingredients for potpourri
all through the gardening season,
harvesting when flowers and leaves
are at their peak. Dry them according to the methods outlined
in pages 30–31. Store each type of
foliage or bloom in separate plastic
bags until you're ready to blend.
Just be sure that all leaves and
flowers are completely dry before
you start mixing them. Moldy
petals or leaves can spoil the
whole batch.

When you make dry potpourri
that will be displayed, add some
small whole blooms dried by one
of the desiccants (see page 31) for
bright touches of color. Collect
and dry berries, cones or other
decorative materials from the garden to add interest to the mixture.

Potpourri made by the dry
method is most attractive stored
in clear glass where you can see
all the ingredients. But you can
use any container for display. A

Sachet notions

cover keeps the mixture fresh
much longer. Just remove it when
you want to release the scent. If
you prefer, you can store the fin-
ished products in plastic bags or
jars and pour out a little into bowls
or baskets to add fragrance to the
air. The scent will last a few weeks
or perhaps as long as one or two
months when constantly exposed
to the air.

Sachets
Sachets are little bags or envelopes filled with dried potpourri.
Traditionally, they are added to
clothes drawers, linen closets,
sweater boxes or anywhere you
want a fresh clean scent.

To make old-fashioned sachets,
wrap potpourri inside pretty hand-
kerchiefs or squares of very thin
fabric and tie into little balls or fold
into interesting shapes. Finish off
with bits of lace and ribbons or
maybe a dried flower.

If you want sachets that lie flat,
make bags or envelopes first, crush
the potpourri into a fine powder
and fill the little envelope. Stitch
closed and add lace, ribbons, applique or other decorative touches.
With a little imagination you can
create beautiful sachets to keep
or give.

If you'd like sachets that repel
moths, stuff with southernwood,
wormwood, thyme, lavender, santolina or tansy. Lay or tie the bags
around winter garments in storage.

If you want a pillow for napping, make a large envelope of a
soft fabric and stuff part of it or a
quilted section or an applique with
the potpourri. If you have lots of
herbs, stuff the whole pillow. Herb-

al pillows are great gifts for per-
sons confined to bed. What could
be more pleasant than resting
your head on a scented pillow
that transports you to the garden
or other pleasures?

When you make sachets don't
forget the cats. Dried catnip leaves
can be stuffed into little fabric
mice or other fantasy creatures
to bring hours of delight to your
own pets or those of friends.

Tussie Mussies
The Elizabethans carried little
nosegays of fresh herbs and flowers known as tussie mussies to
overpower objectionable odors. It
became the custom to present the
little bouquets in silvered water
tubes as personal expressions of
sentiments. Different plants held
special meanings in the language
of flowers (see page 76).

Today the little herbal bouquets
are sometimes carried by brides or
given on special days. Made from
fresh or dried herbal materials
they're also useful as decorative
potpourris for tabletops or displayed in little vases.

Start with a circle or border of
scented leaves such as rose geranium. Add sprigs of herbs to fill
the center and accent with flowers.
Tie it all together with a bit of ribbon. Add a collar of lace if you

Tussie Mussies

like. Make the bouquet from fresh
materials and let it dry naturally in
a warm dry place. Or start with
dried sprigs of herbs and flowers,
or combine with fresh parts, and
wire it all together. Sprinkle with a
bit of orrisroot or other potpourri
fixative and add a few drops of
fragrant oils to preserve the natural scents longer.

Pomander Balls

Old-fashioned pomander balls are simply fruits studded with whole cloves and dried. They're natural air fresheners and can be hung in the closet to repel moths. But even if they served no practical purposes, pomanders would still be popular, especially during the winter holiday season when they're used as tree ornaments and place-card holders, stacked to form table-top trees or given as gifts.

Select perfect pieces of fruit. Oranges are the most popular, but apples, grapefruit, lemons, limes, pears, even kumquats can be used to make balls of various shapes and sizes. Tradition calls for studding the fruit all over closely with whole cloves. As the fruit dries the skin shrinks and draws the cloves closer together. Today many people who make pomanders prefer to save time and add the cloves in rows or patterns or scatter them over the surface leaving some of the fruit skin showing. These areas can be left plain when dried or decorated with small dried flowers or sprigs of herbs or seed head. Always buy good quality whole cloves that are strongly scented.

Holding the fruit in one hand, make a tiny hole in the skin with a nail, skewer or any handy sharp instrument. Press a clove all the way into the hole with your finger. Finish the studding the same day you start before the drying begins.

Many people roll the studded fruit in orrisroot or ground allspice, cinnamon, cloves or nutmeg, cardamom or musk.

If you plan to hang the pomander, insert a skewer, metal knitting needle or straight piece of clothes hanger wire completely through the fruit. As it dries, turn the fruit on the wire regularly to keep it from sticking. When dried, thread it with a length of ribbon, yarn or cord using a crochet hook to work the material through the hole. Tie one end into a knot or bow to keep the ball from slipping off.

Place the pomander in a warm, sunny place to dry for a week or so. Turn it from time to time toward the sun so it will dry evenly. If you're in a big hurry, place the pomander on a baking sheet in an oven that has a pilot light, leaving the door open until the fruit has dried. Do not turn on the heat.

Incenses

The burning of herbs and spices freshens stale air and masks unpleasant household or pet odors. You can purchase powders, sticks and cones in many herbal and spicy scents. Or simply sprinkle powdered herbs and spices on pieces of lighted charcoal in an incense burner or small dish.

A popular recipe originating in the Middle Ages calls for one part myrrh, 5 parts frankincense and 2 parts benzoin mixed together and sprinkled on burning charcoal.

For a subtle long-lasting incense put several pieces of frankincense, myrrh, benzoin or other fragrant gum in a shallow metal container on a stove burner with the heat set as low as possible. As the gum melts, the clean, slightly spicy fragrance penetrates every corner.

Scented Candles

The fragrance of herbs and spices fills the air when candles containing plant parts or their essential oils are burned. Molds for homemade candles can be fashioned from heavy-duty food containers, milk cartons, tin cans, paté and salad molds or other household containers that will hold hot wax.

Melt pieces of leftover unscented candles or paraffin wax blocks over hot water in a double boiler. Add several drops of essential oils of herbs and spices of one kind or mixed, or stir in crushed leaves, petals and spices. For strongly scented candles combine both oils and plant materials. Add pieces of wax crayons for color.

To make the wick, dip a string that's several inches longer than the mold into the hot wax, leaving a few inches of one end unwaxed. Remove and pull taut to straighten. Tie the unwaxed end to a long pencil or stick, position the string down the center of the mold and rest the pencil or stick across the top of the mold. Pour the melted wax around the wick.

Pour the hot wax into the mold, adding whole leaves, petals and spices for more fragrance. You may choose to create a layered look of varied colors by pouring small portions of one color, letting it cool and partially harden, then adding another color.

Allow the candle to harden completely before removing from the mold and trimming the wick. If you used a paper mold, just tear it away. Run hot water over the outside of metal molds.

Clove-studded citrus fruits keep their spicy scents for years. A basketful of eucalyptus pods adds another fragrance.

Scented Oils and Perfumes

Many of the commercially available "essential" oils of plants and flowers are actually synthetically made from chemical residues. The fragrance is almost the same.

To make your own oils at home, you'll need an odorless corn, olive, or safflower oil, although pure melted lard will do. Gather any fragrant fresh leaves or flowers or select a dried spice and fill a wide-mouthed container. Cover with the oil and let stand for 24 hours. Strain through 2 layers of cheesecloth, squeezing to release every drop. Refill the container with more of the fresh or dried material and pour the oil over again. Repeat this straining and pouring every day for 1 to 3 weeks, or until the oil is strongly aromatic. Keep the container in a warm and preferably sunny place throughout the period. When the oil alone is fragrant, strain into little bottles and seal tightly. Homemade fragrance doesn't last long without one of the expensive perfume fixatives such as musk, civet, ambergris or castoreum (available from some pharmacies and mail-order suppliers).

Use the oil as is for bath oil or body scent, or blend with alcohol to create perfume, or use as an additive in potpourri, cosmetics, candles or soaps.

Herbal Oil Massage

A very simple infused oil for body massage can be made by adding 4 ounces mixed herbs to 1 quart mixed vegetable oils or fine olive oil. Leave in a warm place for 2 weeks, then strain through cheesecloth and add up to 1 ounce essential oils. Bottle and label. Use soon or refrigerate to prevent spoilage.

For an easy massage oil start with one quart pure vegetable oils, one kind or mixed. Add ½ ounce of your favorite scented essential oils of herbs or spices, one kind or mixed. Shake well and allow to sit for a few days until fragrance develops.

Perfume

To create your own perfume, mix scented oil, one kind or several with compatible fragrances, with an equal portion of unscented, pure ethyl or rectified alcohol in a tightly closed bottle or jar. Shake together very thoroughly every day for about 2 weeks. Then allow the oil and alcohol to separate naturally. Pour off the oil and use for other purposes. Funnel the remaining alcohol, now perfume, into a little bottle and cap tightly.

An alternate method is to start with the pure alcohol instead of oil and pour it over the fresh herbs or flowers. Follow the same procedure of squeezing and adding fresh ingredients daily until the desired scent is reached. Secure the scent by adding fixative.

Scented Baths and Splashes

A leisurely bath in herbal water does a lot for the tired body and soul. A simple mixture can be concocted by simmering a handful of fresh or dried herbs, flowers and spices in a quart of water for 15 to 20 minutes. Let stand for 30 minutes more to fully develop scents, then strain into hot bath water. Or add a sprinkling of essential oils of herbs, spices or flowers.

You can make herbal bags of dried leaves and flowers to drop into bath water, hang under the tap while the water draws or use as a washcloth. Just tie up dried herbs and flowers in cheesecloth, muslin or linen bags. An old French recipe combines leaves of peppermint, sage, rosemary and thyme with the flowers of chamomile. Other good choices for herbal bathing include lemon balm, bay, calendula, comfrey, lavender, pennyroyal, oregano, rose petals or any of the plants suitable for potpourri. Make up several bags at a time and store in an airtight container. For special gifts, pack several herbal bath bags into a basket or package along with a loofa

sponge, some herbal soaps and perhaps a towel set.

After-shower Splash

Create an alcohol splash as follows:

In a crock or glass container, place fresh or dried leaves of mint, sage, rosemary, lemon balm, seeds of anise or fennel, flowers of lavender or roses, broken pieces of cinnamon or any similar combination of herbs and spices you find appealing. Cover with grain alcohol or high-proof vodka. Let the mixture stand for about two weeks, then filter through a double layer of cheesecloth or coffee filter paper. Bottle one part of the scented alcohol with two parts water.

Shake well and splash on after bathing or showering or have a friend treat you to an herbal rub-down after a hard day's work in your garden. The fragrant alcohol is relaxing to the body and stimulating to the spirit.

Garden Fresh Soaps

Washing with soaps that smell of the herb garden is an invigorating experience. Enjoy all the fragrances of spices and herbs whether you buy soaps from organic shops or make them yourself.

Soap made from bars or left-over scraps of unscented castile or glycerin soaps is quite easy. Just cut the scraps into small pieces and add a little hot water in a saucepan. Pour in drops of essential oils of herbs and spices to create a scent you like. Dissolve the soap over a low heat and pour the hot liquid into molds to harden.

Individual salad molds, tin cans and plastic and paper cartons make good molds for soaps. Large portions of soap can be made in milk cartons then sliced into bars when hardened. Let your soaps sit for several days in the air to hard-

en before using.

You might pour some of the soap solution into old fashioned shaving mugs and let harden. A soap-filled mug is a great gift, along with a shaving brush.

Consult recipes for lye-based homemade soaps and add your own herbs and spices to the mixture. (See Ortho's *12 Months Harvest,* page 79, or *All About Roses,* pages 88 and 89.)

Many herbalists offer plant parts that contain saponins (glucosides that produce a soapy lather) as substitutes. You might enjoy trying roots of the California soap plant, soap tree yucca, soapwort, salt-bush or Spanish bayonet, or the leaves of papaya and guaiac, as well as fruits of soap pod and wild gourd. They'll produce lather when activated in warm soft water. People who use them recommend them for washing delicate fabrics. Check nearby herb shops or mail-order sources for availability.

Skin and Hair Care

A quick check of commercially available products for the skin and hair reveals that herbs are used freely. You can duplicate many of these products at home with garden fresh or dried herbs. There are arguments on both sides as to whether the herbs actually serve any practical purposes in the care of skin and hair. Even if they are no more than a refreshing fragrance, they're certainly welcomed additions to these cosmetic aids.

Herbal Steam Facial
Steaming is one of the best ways to cleanse the skin. The addition of herbs to the hot steam supposedly helps cleanse, stimulate, soothe and tighten the skin, remove impurities and aid in blemish control. At the very least they are delightful to the senses.

Pour boiling water over fresh or dried herbs in a basin and make a tent of a towel to hold over your head. Let the steam soak your face for 10 minutes or as long as you can stand the heat. Chamomile flowers are the most popular for steam facials. Other possibilities are elder flowers, lime, strawberry leaves, yarrow, lady's mantle, fennel, comfrey, roses, peppermint, horsetail, nettle, rosemary. Use alone or in combinations.

There are many cleansers and cosmetics that can be made at home using simple ingredients available from the pharmacy or mail-order suppliers combined with herbs, either fresh or dried.

Cold Cream
To make your own cold cream, blend 1 part pure olive oil with 4 parts pure solid vegetable shortening. Add several drops of tincture of benzoin and fragrant herbal oils. An easy alternative starts with storebought *unscented* cold cream. Just blend in essential oils.

Cleansing Cream
Another cleansing cream calls for melting 1 part white wax with 4 parts avocado or almond oil. Then add 1 part rose or other flower water, 2 parts aloe gel and a few drops of fragrant oils a little at a time, beating constantly with a fork or in a blender. When mixed pour into jars.

Skin Cleanser
Rose water and glycerin is a traditional skin cleanser. It's concocted by mixing equal portions of glycerin with rose water. Heat just to boiling and store in tightly closed bottles or jars.

Herbal Astringents
Herbal astringents are used to close skin pores, remove excess oils and as aftershave lotions. Begin with an herb extract made by steeping the chosen herb in a jar of pure ethyl alcohol. Suggested astringent herbs include chamomile, bayberry bark, sage, nettle, lady's mantle and yarrow. Strain after one week and add more of the herb. After the second week, strain through doubled cheesecloth and bottle. To each ¼ cup of herb extract, add ½ cup witch hazel, 2 teaspoons glycerine, ½ teaspoon powdered boric acid and ½ teaspoon tincture of benzoin. For an added tingle add 1 teaspoon peppermint extract. Cap tightly; shake before using.

Hand Cream
An excellent hand cream can be created from simple ingredients in five minutes time. Start by squeezing a lemon and straining through cheesecloth. Pour juice into a measuring cup and add an equal amount of almond oil. In a small pan put a thin piece of beeswax (about 1 teaspoon). Add a bit of the almond oil that has collected above the lemon juice in the measuring cup. Place over medium heat and gently shake the pot for about 30 seconds. Take off heat so that wax melts but does not burn. Add remaining almond-lemon mixture. Heat, shake, and stir with a wooden spoon until wax has completely melted. Remove from heat. Stir until cool with wooden spoon. Add 1 drop lemon oil for every ounce of cream (about 3 drops). Stir again and transfer to cream jar or bottle. Cap. Shake every few minutes until cream is completely cold.

Mouthwash
A simple breath freshening mouthwash can be made from a strong peppermint tea or by steeping equal portions of mint, anise and rosemary in boiling water. Strain and store in a tightly capped bottle. For a spicy version grind your own blend of cloves, caraway, cinnamon and nutmeg in a mortar and pestle. Combine the spice mixture with equal part sherry,

add a few drops of tincture of myrrh, peppermint or lavender and let stand for several days. To use pour a few drops into a glass of water.

Shampoo

Create your own special shampoo blend with a base of liquid castile soap available from organic stores. Add a strong infusion or tea of selected herbs and stir together over low heat until the soap melts and the shampoo is well blended. Add essential herb or spice oils for extra fragrance. To save steps start with a commercial avocado, castile or coconut shampoo and add the herbal infusion and scents. Store in tightly closed bottles. The following herbs are recommended by many herbalists as shampoo additives:

Light hair/calendula, chamomile, great mullein or orange flowers, nettle, orrisroot, turmeric

Dark hair/rosemary, sage, cloves, Chinese cinnamon, lavender, sassafras, mint, marjoram, yarrow

Red hair/calendula and hibiscus flowers, witch hazel bark, cloves

Oily hair/lemongrass, orrisroot, peppermint, witch hazel

Dry hair/citrus peel, comfrey, elder flowers, red clover

Herbal Protein Shampoo

San Francisco herbalist Jeanne Rose created a special herbal protein shampoo for us.

2   tablespoons Irish moss
½   cup each chamomile and
     calendula flowers, fresh or
     dried
¼   cup orange peel, fresh or
     dried
¼   cup orrisroot
4½ cups water
¾   cup shaved castile soaplets
     A few drops essential oils of
     your choice dissolved in
     ½ ounce tincture of benzoin

Mix herbs together and boil in water in an enamel pot for about 5 minutes. Turn off heat and let steep. Meanwhile, measure soap on a postal scale and pour into an enamel bowl. Strain herbs through cheesecloth or muslin into the soap. Gently beat until soap is dissolved, heating if necessary. Pour into quart container, add oils and shake. Cap and label.

Hair Rinse

A simple hair rinse can be easily made by adding 1 cup of boiling water to 3 to 4 tablespoons herbs and simmering gently for several minutes. Strain and blend with 1 cup cold bottled "spring" water. Pour over shampooed hair. Work it through the hair, squeeze out excess and dry. Use the same herbs as suggested for shampoos, adding any others that have appealing fragrances.

Natural Hair Colors

The ancient Egyptians and their neighbors used henna to smooth and color the hair. Today it's regaining popularity. Henna coats each hair shaft to make the hair appear thicker as it smooths the cuticle layer. Many people who want these qualities without changing hair color use natural henna. Colored henna is available in shades from black, through brown, mahogany, to deep red. It's difficult to control the evenness of the color and takes a lot of experimentation at home, so colored henna is best applied by a professional. Herbal cosmeticians recommend natural henna.

However, if you want to try it yourself, start with about 2 cups henna powder and add hot water to form a thick paste. A teaspoon of vinegar helps release the dye. Stir the paste well and let it stand while you shampoo the hair. When applying henna wear rubber gloves to avoid staining hands and nails. Wrap the hairline in cotton to prevent dripping. Apply to sections of the hair with a stiff brush, painting both sides of the hair. When completed, cover the head with a plastic bag and keep it on for ½ to 1½ hours. Rinse until water comes clear.

Practitioners of the art of natural cosmetics suggest a wide range of herbal parts for coloring. Natural hair colors for dark hair include crushed walnut shells, sandalwood, redwood bark, brazilwood and elder berries. To brighten dull dark hair, apply rosemary or southernwood. To brighten light colored hair apply chamomile, calendula, great mullein leaves or lemon peel. To darken gray hair make a decoction of sage, bay laurel, marjoram and wood betony.

Herbal Makeup

Herbal makeup adds a very natural touch of color to highlight healthy skin. Here are some easy ones for the home herbalist to prepare. Start with small quantities and experiment with the amounts of herbs used to create desired colors. A collection of herbal makeup items, along with skin and hair care products packed into a kit, bag, basket or tray is a refreshing way to share the harvest of your garden with special friends.

Lipstick

Alkanet root is the basis for a blush or lipstick in a pot. Mix 2 tablespoons of the root in ½ cup sesame oil and let stand for about 2 weeks. Then melt 4 tablespoons beeswax in a saucepan and add the strained oil mixture. Beat until cold and store in small jars.

Eye Shadow

Eye shadows can be made by heating 1 part fresh herb to 4 parts pure oil until the oil is well colored. Add 1 part beeswax to the oil and heat until melted. Beat until cold and pack into small containers. For lavender shadow use black malva flowers combined with alkanet. For green eye shadow use parsley. For yellow shadow start with calendula petals. Apply a strong decoction of sage boiled in a black cast iron pot to darken the eyebrows.

Nail Polish

A softly colored nail polish can be made from henna powder simply by adding hot water to form a thin paste. Paint onto nails with a small brush and let dry. Rinse with cold water.

Decorating with Herbs and Spices

In addition to the beauty of herb plants in the indoor/outdoor landscape, preserved plant forms can be used in many ways to add color and warmth to a home.

Perhaps the easiest way to display garden materials is in bouquets of dried flowers and foliages that have been preserved by one of the methods described on pages 30–33.

Dried Bouquets

Especially pretty when dried are leaves of eucalyptus, horehound, lamb's ears, sage, mints and oregano; the seed pods of dill and fennel, and rose hips; and flowers of alliums, bergamot, calendula, dock, goldenrod, roses, safflower, tansy, and wormwood. Many other plants are attractive when dried. Experiment with the different plant parts and preserving techniques.

Flowers with strong stiff stems will stand just as they are. Others will need lengths of stiff florist's wire attached to the base of the flower, seed head or the foliage clump. Bend the wire back at the length you want for the stem. Holding the attached blossom or head securely, use your other hand to wrap the remaining length several times around the short remaining stem or foliage clump. For roses, calendulas and other flowers with fat bases, remove the stems and insert the wire through the base of the flower.

Beginning at the flower or pod base or the end of the foliage, wrap florist's tape tightly to cover the wire, stretching as you wrap downward. A shade of brown or drab green tape looks best with dried flowers and leaves.

Cut a piece of styrofoam to fill the base of the container or basket

Bouquets of dried herbal flowers, seed heads and foliages can add color to the interior all year long. The rich autumnal hues of yarrow, safflowers, dock, cress and other materials in the crock were preserved by hang drying. Pastel shades work best when dried in a desiccant (see page 31). Keep dried bouquets out of direct sunlight to preserve color longer. Professional florists advocate spraying with a thin coat of hair lacquer to prevent shedding.

selected for the bouquet. If necessary secure the foam to the bottom of the container with sticky floral adhesive. If you can see the styrofoam, cover it with dried green moss. Push the flower stems or wires into the foam. A coating of hair spray over the completed bouquet will help keep the dried materials together. To maintain as much color as possible keep the bouquet away from strong sunlight.

Miniature Bouquets

Some people enjoy making miniature bouquets and displaying them underneath a glass dome or inside a deep shadowbox frame.

The little bouquets known as tussie mussies are charming accents for bedside tables, powder rooms or other small areas. Both tussie mussies and containers of colorful potpourri are decorative as well as practical air fresheners. The little herbal bouquets and potpourri are charming gifts, too. See page 67 for instructions.

Herb and Spice Wreaths

A variation of the dried bouquet is the herb and spice wreath for winter holiday decoration. Use a wire wreath frame from the florist as an anchor for sprigs of dried herbs. Wire them to the frame to make a lush base. Grey or silver herb foliage is especially pretty as the base. Add colorful flowers, seed heads and pods, cones and berries to complete the design. Keep the color scheme monochromatic, add one complementary or contrasting color, or create a fantasy of mixed hues. The addition of a bow and streamers is a matter of personal taste. For a simpler wreath design select only one type of foliage or seed head and fashion into a circle.

Fragrant herbal wreaths are attractive on doors, windows or walls, especially in dining areas or kitchens. They are equally attractive on tabletops where they can ring candles or punch bowls for a party.

After the holidays you can hang the wreath near the stove to use the sprigs in cooking. Or you can spray it with hair spray and store away in a large plastic bag for use again next year. Friends will appreciate wreaths as gifts.

Bay Leaf Wreath

Much-appreciated holiday gifts are bay leaf wreaths that can be hung in the kitchen and used all year. Wrap a round styrofoam wreath base in velvet ribbon or strips of burlap. Using ordinary sewing pins, attach bay leaves thickly over the base, continually overlapping the ends of the leaves to hide it and the pins. Add a flat simple velvet or grosgrain ribbon bow.

Garlands

Instead of turning dried herbs and flowers into circular wreaths you may enjoy making a long garland to festoon a stairway, mantle or buffet table. Tie the wired floral and foliage pieces to a long piece of wire or heavy cord cut to any desired length. Begin with a base of herb foliage, then add flowers, berries and other decorative accents as in making wreaths.

Garlic Braids

Don't forget strings of braided garlic, peppers and onions that are described on page 33 for year-round decorations. They're colorful accents for kitchen and dining areas.

Other Christmas Decorations

Sprigs of herbs and flowers are pretty on the Christmas tree. Tie them into little nosegays and add to the tree along with other traditional ornaments. An entire tree can be decorated with dried garden plants. First insert sprays of delicate looking flowers or seed heads to completely fill in all the spaces between tree branches. Next add colorful flowers, pomander balls, pods and other dried materials as bold accents. Such a tree takes a lot of dried materials and time, but the results are spectacular and highly aromatic. Use the same idea and techniques to make a small tabletop tree for a party centerpiece.

If you'd like a more permanent herbal tree, cover an 18-inch styrofoam cone with ribbon or green moss held in place with fern pins or bent pieces of wire. Cover the cone with delicate dried seed heads or airy flowers. Then add larger flowers and herb sprigs, along with cones and berries for accents. The tree can be sprayed with hair lacquer and stored away in plastic bags for another year.

The Language of Herbs and Spices

Agrimony: thankfulness, gratitude
Allspice: compassion
Aloe: grief, affection
Angelica: inspiration
Balm: sympathy
Barberry: sourness, sharpness, ill temper
Basil: hatred
Basil, sweet: good wishes
Bay leaf: I change but in death
Bay tree: glory
Bay wreath: reward of merit
Betony: surprise
Birch: meekness
Borage: bluntness
Burdock: importunity, touch me not
Carnation, red: alas for my heart
Carnation, striped: refusal
Carnation, yellow: disdain
Chamomile: energy in adversity
Cloves: dignity
Clover, red: industry
Coltsfoot: justice shall be done
Columbine: folly
Coriander: concealed merit
Cornflower: single blessedness
Cowslip: pensiveness, winning grace
Cress: stability
Dandelion: oracle
Dittany of Crete: birth
Dock: patience
Fennel: worthy of all praise
Foxglove: insincerity
Fumitory: spleen
Chervil: sincerity
Geranium, nutmeg: an unexpected meeting
Geranium, rose: preference

Goldenrod: precaution, encouragement
Heliotrope: devotion
Hibiscus: delicate beauty
Hop: injustice
Hyssop: cleanliness
Lavender: distrust
Marjoram: blushes
Mint: virtue
Myrrh: gladness
Myrtle: love
Nasturtium: patriotism
Parsley: festivity
Pennyroyal: flee away
Peppermint: warmth of feeling
Pink: boldness
Rose: love
Rose, damask: brilliant complexion
Rose, musk: charming
Rosebud, red: pure and lovely
Rosebud, white: girlhood and a heart ignorant of love
Rosemary: remembrance
Rue: disdain
Saffron crocus: mirth
Sage: domestic virtue or esteem
Sorrel: affection
Southernwood: jest, banter
Spearmint: warmth of sentiment
Speedwell: female fidelity
Sunflower: haughtiness
Tansy: I declare war against you
Thyme: activity
Valerian: an accommodating disposition
Vervain: enchantment
Violet, sweet: modesty
Witch hazel: a spell
Wormwood: absence

Natural Notes and Pictures

Foliages and flowers from the herb garden can be turned into cards and mounted pictures that you'll enjoy making, keeping and giving.

Select perfect leaves and flowers from your garden and press them so they aren't touching between sheets of blotting paper or unprinted news stock weighted down by heavy books. Press small blooms whole, but separate the petals of larger or thicker flowers and press each separately. When dry, in about four or five weeks, gently lift off the pages with tweezers and store the pressed material between sheets of waxed paper until ready to make designs. Dry a large variety of materials this way so you'll have good choices when you create projects later.

Flower Press
For a more professional way of pressing plant parts, buy a flower press from the hobby store or build your own simple version: Cut 2 pieces of heavy plywood 1 foot square and drill holes an inch from each corner. Cut several sheets of corrugated cardboard and blotting paper to fit inside, cutting off the corners to allow room for screws to be inserted through the corner holes.

Arrange the petals, flowers and leaves on a piece of blotter so the plants don't touch. Cover with another blotter, slip between a pair of cardboard sheets. Continue until all the plant parts are accommodated, then put the whole stack between the plywood. Insert 3 to 4-inch screws and fasten tightly with wing nuts. Store for a month or until the plants are crisp.

When the materials are completely dry, remove with tweezers and store between waxed paper.

You can form a design of the petals and leaves on plain notecards and envelopes from the stationery store. Glue each petal, flower or leaf in place with thinned rubber cement. Burnish by covering with tissue paper and rubbing the surface with your finger or a flat stick. When the glue dries carefully rub off any excess from around the edges of the plant.

Smaller versions of notecards make attractive gift tags.

Use the pressed materials to illustrate pages of your garden diary or create a little book of herbs and spices with plant identifications (see instructions below).

Take the idea a step further and make a book using the centuries-old "language of flowers." See our listing of plants from the herb garden and their old-fashioned meanings. Decorate the pages of the book with flowers and leaves of the plant, write in the common and botanical names, along with the sentiment expressed in the old floral language. Your creation is bound to become a treasured gift —or a family keepsake.

Pressed flowers and leaves can be formed into larger designs and glued to artists' mounting board, then framed under glass. An alternate method is to glue the plant pieces directly onto the back side of glass or lucite box frames available from hobby shops. Hang your pictures away from sunlight to preserve colors.

The Gardener's Diary

Sentimental and serious gardeners enjoy keeping a record of plants in the herb garden: sources of seeds or cuttings, location in the garden, culture, plant response and yearly harvest.

To make the diary distinctive you might want to buy a leather or clothbound book with blank pages. Or cover an inexpensive sketchbook with fabric you like. If you can draw, sketch or watercolor the plant alongside your record page. Or add pressed leaves and petals from the plant (see above).

Decorate diary pages with pressed herbs.

The Almost Forgotten Art of Natural Dyeing

Strong infusions of almost any herbs boiled in water can be used in coloring natural fabrics: cotton, linen, silk or, most satisfactorily, wool. Of course the dyes from some plants are more readily absorbed than others by the fibers. See below for a partial listing of plants and colors.

Don't expect the bright colors of synthetic dyes. Natural dyes are subtle, bordering on drab. Hues will vary according to where and how the plant grew, the strength of the dye solution, whether the dye is made from fresh or dried plant parts and the type of mordant (dye-setting compound) used.

Prior to the actual dyeing, it's necessary to treat the fabric in a mordant to set the dye in the fibers. Alum is the most commonly used mordant, but acetic acid, ammonia, chrome, tin and iron chemicals are also used.

The mordanting and dyeing procedure varies with the fabric, plant material and mordant selected. Our space doesn't permit detailed instructions, but there are several books devoted to dyeing if you wish to pursue the hobby.

Herbal Colors:

Reds/alkanet roots, bloodroot roots, bedstraw roots, madder roots, oregano leaves, tea leaves

Oranges/henna leaves, lily-of-the-valley leaves, onion skins, sorrel leaves, tansy shoots

Yellows/agrimony leaves and flowers, barberry stems and roots, calendula flowers, dyer's broom tops, fustic wood, goldenrod blooms, saffron crocus blooms, St. John's Wort flowers, turmeric roots, yarrow flowers

Violet/hibiscus flowers, oregano leaves

Blue/cornflowers, elecampane roots, hollyhock flowers, wild indigo branches

Green/coltsfoot leaves, dyer's broom tops, fumitory leaves, hyssop leaves, larkspur flowers, onion skins, sorrel leaves, sweet cicely stems and leaves

Brown/hibiscus flowers, juniper berries, tea leaves

Grey/blackberry shoots

Black/barberry leaves, yellow dock roots

The world of herbs and spices becomes a world of crafts—pomander balls, jars of potpourri and herbal teas, dozens of dried specimens for mid-winter bouquets.

Illustrated Guide to Herbs and Spices

More than 160 herbs and spices are available in preserved forms from market shelves, mail order herbalists, or to grow and preserve at home.

Shown on the following pages are herbs and spices that are available in some preserved form from commercial suppliers. The many other herbs that are available are generally used in medicines and home remedies. We choose to show only those that have more universal appeal and safe uses.

Many of these plants can be grown and preserved at home — note our recommendations under *Home garden* in the notes accompanying each picture. In some cases, only certain regions or climates will do. Other herbs can be grown anywhere but are not recommended for homegrowing because of their weedy appearance and wild growth habits. "Indoors/outdoors" means that the plants can be grown in either or can be rotated with the seasons. Plants recommended for indoors can be grown under artificial lighting. Some plants can be homegrown yet will never produce enough of the useful portion to do much good. These are suggested as ornamentals only.

We give you both common and botanical names. Some plants go by several common names and our first listing is the one we judge most widely known. We used the new *Hortus Third,* recognized authority in horticultural circles, for the nomenclature and spelling of botanical names. As you read through the list you'll see some names repeatedly, a result of the

Helen Ganaway's apothecary jars contain common and exotic herbs.

Herbs and spices come from all parts of plants: roots, pods, seeds, bark, leaves, flowers and berries.

original usage of the plant. For example, *officinalis* or *officinale* means that the plant was used for medicinal purposes at the time it was classified. Likewise, *tinctoria* indicates that the plant was mainly used as a dye and *odorata* suggests a sweet-smelling plant. Even though a plant's use has changed, the name remains the same.

A few botanical names have been reassigned or plants have been reclassified in the new *Hortus,* so you may find a few names that appear to be wrong if you judge by older guides. Our basic purpose in using the newest botanical identity is to help you when you want to locate a particular plant — common names vary from region to region but the language of horticulture remains consistent, if not constant. And it's fun to learn as many basic names as you can

along the way. Pronunciation is exactly as the word looks: just sound out each syllable.

In addition to naming names, we'll tell you where the plants originated. Many of the spices are still produced commercially in the same regions while others have crossed oceans to similar climates. Most of the commercially available herbs in the United States come from California or the New England states. A few are imported, mainly from Latin America, Europe and the Orient.

In our listing, *Parts* refers to the portion of the plant used: roots, stems, bark, leaves, flowers, seeds. *Form* describes how the parts are used: whole seeds or cut leaves, for example.

Flavor or *Scent* refers to the taste or aroma of the useful plant part. In many cases the unique flavor or scent of an herb or spice has itself become a description, such as licorice, garlic or vanilla.

Some preserved herbs and spices are available in more than one form and the choice depends on your individual preferences and how you plan to use the herb or spice. In the case of herbs, it's usually best to obtain and store them in as whole a form as possible and pulverize as needed.

Under *Uses* we briefly mention the main ways that the plant's parts are used: culinary, cosmetics, fragrance.

Mail order sources for seeds and plants, and suppliers of preserved herbs and spices are listed on page 93.

Agrimony.
Church steeples, cocklebur.
Agrimonia eupatoria.
Origin: Europe, North Africa, Western Asia
Parts: Leaves, flowers
Scent: Apricot
Form: Cut
Uses: Dye, fragrance
Home garden: Outdoors

Alfalfa.
Medicago sativa.
Origin: Southwest Asia
Parts: Sprouted seeds, leaves
Flavor: Delicate
Form: Whole seed, cut leaves
Uses: Culinary, tea (leaves)
Home garden: Indoors (sprouts)

Alkanet.
Bugloss.
Anchusa officinalis.
Origin: Europe, Asia Minor
Parts: Rootbark
Form: Pieces
Uses: Dye, furniture polish
Home garden: Outdoors

Allspice.
Pimenta dioica.
Origin: West Indies, Latin America
Parts: Berries
Flavor: Pungent
Form: Whole, ground
Uses: Culinary
Home garden: Not recommended

Aloe vera.
Aloe barbadensis.
Origin: Netherlands Antilles
Parts: Fleshy leaves
Flavor: Bitter
Form: Resin
Uses: Skin care
Home garden: Indoors/ outdoors, container.

Angelica.
Archangel.
Angelica species.
Origin: Europe, Asia
Parts: Stalks, seeds, roots
Flavor: Bitter
Form: Pieces and seed, candied stalk
Uses: Culinary, tea
Home garden: Outdoors

Anise.
Pimpinella anisum.
Origin: Greece, Middle East
Parts: Seeds
Flavor: Sweet, licorice
Form: Whole, candied
Uses: Culinary, liqueur, cosmetics
Home garden: Outdoors, difficult in north

Annatto.
Bixa orellana.
Origin: Florida
Parts: Seeds
Form: Whole
Uses: Dye, food coloring
Home garden: Not recommended

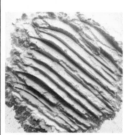

Arrowroot.
Maranta arundinacea.
Origin: West Indies
Parts: Rhizomes
Flavor: Tasteless
Form: Powdered
Uses: Culinary
Home garden: Indoors as ornamental

Asparagus.
Asparagus officinalis.
Origin: Europe, North Africa, Asia
Parts: Seeds, roots
Form: Whole seed, cut root
Uses: Coffee substitute (seed), tea (root)
Home garden: Outdoors

Barberry.
Jaundice berry.
Berberis vulgaris.
Origin: Europe
Parts: Roots
Form: Cut
Uses: Dye
Home garden: Outdoors

Basil.
Ocimum basilicum.
Origin: Tropical Africa
Parts: Leaves
Flavor: Sweet
Form: Cut
Uses: Culinary
Home garden: Indoors/ outdoors

Bay.
Laurus nobilis.
Origin: Mediterranean
Parts: Leaves
Flavor: Sweet, spicy
Form: Whole, crushed
Uses: Culinary, fragrance
Home garden: Indoors/ outdoors
California bay *(Umbellularia californica)* often substituted

Bayberry.
Myrica pensylvanica.
Origin: North America
Parts: Rootbark
Scent: Evergreen
Form: Cut
Uses: Candlemaking, fragrance
Home garden: Outdoors

Bergamot, wild.
Horsemint.
Monarda punctata.
Origin: North America
Parts: Leaves
Flavor: Minty
Form: Cut
Uses: Tea, fragrance
Home garden: Outdoors

Birch.

Betula species.

Origin: Northern
Hemisphere
Parts: Bark, leaves
Form: Cut
Uses: Tea
Home garden: Outdoors

Blackberry.

Rubus species.

Origin: North America
Parts: Leaves, roots
Flavor: Mild
Form: Cut
Uses: Tea, dye
Home garden: Outdoors

Bloodroot.

Sanguinaria canadensis.

Origin: North America
Parts: Rhizomes
Form: Cut, ground
Uses: Dye
Home garden: Outdoors

Boneset.

Eupatorim perfoliatum.

Origin: North America
Parts: Leaves
Flavor: Bitter
Form: Crushed
Uses: Tea
Home garden: Outdoors

Borage.

Bee bread, talewort,
cool-tankard.
Borago officinalis.

Origin: Europe, North
Africa
Parts: Leaves, stems,
flowers
Flavor: Cucumber
Form: Cut
Uses: Culinary, tea
Home garden: Outdoors

Burdock.

Beggar's buttons,
cuckold, gobo, harlock.
Arctium lappa.

Origin: Eurasia, North
America
Parts: Roots
Flavor: None
Form: Cut, powdered
Uses: Culinary
Home garden: Outdoors

Calendula.

Marigold, pot marigold.
Calendula officinalis.

Origin: Southern Europe
Parts: Flowers
Flavor: Mild
Form: Petals
Uses: Culinary
Home garden: Indoors/
outdoors

Capers.

Capparis spinosa.

Origin: Mediterranean
Parts: Flower buds
Flavor: Pungent
Form: Pickled
Uses: Culinary
Home garden: Outdoors,
grow as annual in cold
regions

Caraway.

Carum carvi.

Origin: Europe, North
America
Parts: Seeds
Flavor: Licorice
Form: Whole
Uses: Culinary
Home garden: Outdoors
except along coasts

Cardamom.

Elettaria cardamomum.

Origin: India
Parts: Seeds
Flavor: Spicy, pungent
Form: Whole, shelled,
ground (green or
roasted)
Uses: Culinary, fragrance
Home garden: Not
recommended

Carob.

Ceratonia siliqua.

Origin: Eastern
Mediterranean
Parts: Seeds, fruits
Flavor: Chocolatelike
Form: Cut, powdered
(raw or roasted)
Uses: Culinary
Home garden: Outdoors,
not in frost areas

Catnip.

Catmint.
Nepeta cataria.

Origin: Eurasia
Parts: Leaves
Flavor: Sweet, minty
Form: Crushed
Uses: Tea, cat toys
Home garden: Indoors/
outdoors

Cayenne.

Capsicum annuum
Longum Group.

Origin: North and
South America
Parts: Podlike berries
Flavor: Hot
Form: Whole, ground
Uses: Culinary
Home garden: Outdoors

Cedar, red.

Juniperus virginiana.

Origin: North America
Parts: Wood
Scent: Evergreen
Form: Powdered, chips
Uses: Fragrance
Home garden: Outdoors

Celery.

Apium graveolens.

Origin: Worldwide
Parts: Seeds
Flavor: Mild
Form: Whole, ground
Uses: Culinary
Home garden: Outdoors

Chamomile.
Camomile.
Chamaemelum nobile
(Roman), *Matricaria
recutita* (German).
Origin: Western Europe,
Azores, North Africa
Parts: Flowers
Flavor: Applelike
Form: Whole
Uses: Tea, cosmetics,
fragrances
Home garden: Outdoors

Chervil.
Anthriscus cerefolium.
Origin: Europe, Western
Asia
Parts: Leaves
Flavor: Anise-parsley
Form: Crushed
Uses: Culinary
Home garden: Indoors/
outdoors

Chia.
Salvia columbariae.
Origin: Southwest United
States
Parts: Sprouted seeds
Flavor: Delicate
Form: Whole
Uses: Culinary
Home garden: Indoors

Chicory.
Cichorium intybus.
Origin: North Africa,
Europe, Western Asia
Parts: Roots
Flavor: Slightly bitter
Form: Raw or roasted
pieces, ground
Uses: Coffee additive
or substitute
Home garden: Outdoors

Chili pepper.
*Capsicum annuum
Longum Group.*
Origin: North and
South America
Parts: Podlike berries
Flavor: Hot, spicy
Form: Whole, crushed,
ground.
Uses: Culinary
Home garden: Outdoors

Chili powder.
A mixture of ground
chili peppers with herbs
and spices.

Chinese cinnamon.
Cassia bark.
Cinnamomum cassia.
Origin: Burma, China,
Indonesia
Parts: Bark
Flavor: Sweet, spicy
Form: Pieces, ground
Uses: Culinary, fragrance
Home garden: Not
recommended

Chinese Five Spices.
A mixture of ground star
anise, fennel, cinnamon,
cloves and Szechwan
pepper.

Chives.
Allium schoenoprasum.
Origin: Europe, Asia
Parts: Leaves
Flavor: Mild
Form: Chopped
Uses: Culinary
Home garden: Indoors/
outdoors

Chocolate.
Cocoa.
Theobroma cacao.
Origin: Central and
South America
Parts: Seeds
Flavor: Bitter
Form: Roasted, then
powdered or formed
into cakes
Uses: Culinary, beverage
Home garden: Not
recommended

Chrysanthemum.
Garland chrysanthemum,
crown daisy.
*Chrysanthemum
coronarium.*
Origin: Mediterranean,
Orient
Parts: Flowers
Flavor: Mildly pungent
Form: Whole, petals
Uses: Culinary, garnish
Home garden: Outdoors

Cinnamon.
Ceylon cinnamon.
*Cinnamomum
zeylanicum.*
Origin: Ceylon, India
Parts: Bark
Flavor: Sweet, pungent
Form: Pieces, ground
Uses: Culinary, fragrance
Home garden: Not
recommended

Citrus.
Citrus species.
Origin: Asia
Parts: Fruit, flowers
Flavor: Sweet, acidic
Form: Diced or ground
peel, petals
Uses: Culinary, fragrance,
tea
Home garden: Indoors/
outdoors in warm
climates

Cloves.
Syzygium aromaticum.
Origin: Moluccas
(Indonesia)
Parts: Flower buds
Flavor: Pungent, sweet
Form: Whole, ground
Uses: Culinary, fragrance
Home garden: Not
recommended.

Coffee.
Coffea arabica.
Origin: Tropical Africa,
Latin America
Parts: Seeds
Flavor: Unique, slightly
bitter
Form: Roasted whole,
ground
Uses: Beverage, culinary
Home garden: Indoors
or greenhouse as
ornamental

Cola nut.

Cola acuminata.
Origin: Tropical Africa
Parts: Seeds
Flavor: Cola
Form: Pieces, powdered
Uses: Beverage
Home garden: Not recommended

Coltsfoot.

Tussilago farfara.
Origin: Europe, west and north Asia, North Africa
Parts: Leaves
Flavor: Strong
Form: Cut
Uses: Dye, tea, tobacco substitute
Home garden: Not recommended.

Comfrey.

Blackwort, knit-bone.
Symphytum officinale.
Origin: Asia, Europe
Parts: Leaves, root
Flavor: Subtle
Form; Cut root, cut or powdered leaves
Uses: Tea
Home garden: Outdoors

Coriander.

Cilantro, Chinese parsley.
Coriandrum sativum.
Origin: Southern Europe
Parts: Seeds (coriander), leaves (cilantro or Chinese parsley)
Flavor: Sweet, pungent
Form: Leaves cut; seed whole, ground
Uses: Culinary
Home garden: Indoors/outdoors

Cornflower.

Centaurea cyanus.
Origin: Europe, Near East
Parts: Flowers
Form: Cut
Uses: Dye
Home garden: Outdoors

Cubeb.

Piper cubeba.
Origin: Southeast Asia
Parts: Berries
Flavor: Peppery
Form: Whole
Uses: Culinary
Home garden: Not recommended.

Cumin.

Cuminum cyminum.
Origin: Mediterranean
Parts: Seeds
Flavor: Pungent, carawaylike
Form: Whole, ground
Uses: Culinary
Home garden: Outdoors in warm climates

Curry powder.

A mixture of spices, such as fenugreek, turmeric, cumin, mustard seed, cardamom, ginger and peppers ranging from mild to hot, used as seasoning.

Damiana.

Turnera aphrodisiaca.
Origin: Tropical America
Parts: Leaves
Form: Cut
Uses: Tea
Home garden: Not recommended

Dandelion.

Taraxacum officinale.
Origin: Europe, Asia
Parts: Roots, leaves
Flavor: Slightly bitter
Form: Cut leaves, raw or roasted root pieces
Uses: Tea, coffee additive
Home garden: Outdoors if controlled.

Desert tea.

Mormon tea.
Ephedra species.
Origin: Northern Hemisphere
Parts: Leaves
Form: Cut
Uses: Tea
Home garden: Not recommended

Dill.

Anethum graveolens.
Origin: Southwest Asia
Parts: Leaves, seeds
Flavor: Sweet leaves, slightly bitter seeds
Form: Seeds whole, leaves cut
Uses: Culinary
Home garden: Indoors/outdoors

Dittany of Crete.

Hop marjoram.
Origanum dictamnus.
Origin: Greece, Crete
Parts: Leaves
Flavor: Marjoramlike
Form: Crushed
Uses: Tea
Home garden: Indoors/outdoors

Dyer's broom.

Dyer's greenwood.
Genista tinctoria.
Origin: Europe, West Africa
Parts: Tops
Form: Cut
Uses: Dye
Home garden: Outdoors

Elder.

Sambucus species.
Origin: North America
Parts: Flowers, berries, bark, leaves
Flavor: Subtle
Form: Cut leaves and flowers, bark pieces, whole berries
Uses: Culinary, cosmetics, tea
Home garden: Outdoors

Elecampane.

Inula helenium.
Origin: Central America
Parts: Roots
Flavor: Bitter
Form: Cut
Uses: Liqueur flavoring, dye
Home garden: Outdoors

Eucalyptus.

Gum tree.
Eucalyptus species.
Origin: Australia
Parts: Leaves
Scent: Medicinal
Form: Whole or cut leaves
Uses: Fragrance, decoration
Home garden: Outdoors in mild climates

Fennel.

Sweet fennel.
Foeniculum vulgare.
Origin: Southern Europe
Parts: Leaves, seeds
Flavor: Aniselike
Form: Seed whole or powdered, leaves cut
Uses: Culinary
Home garden: Outdoors

Fenugreek.

Trigonella foenum-graecum.
Origin: Southern Europe, Asia
Parts: Seeds
Flavor: Slightly bitter, maplelike
Form: Whole
Uses: Culinary, dye
Home garden: Outdoors

Filé.

A mixture consisting chiefly of ground leaves of *Sassafras albidum* with other herbs and spices; used as a thickener in Creole cookery.

Frankincense.

Boswellia species.
Origin: Asia, Africa
Parts: Resin
Scent: Sweet, spicy
Form: Gum
Uses: Fragrance
Home garden: Not recommended

Fumitory.

Earth smoke.
Fumaria officinalis.
Origin: Northern temperate regions
Parts: Flowering foliage
Form: Cut
Uses: Dye
Home garden: Not recommended

Garam Masala.

A mixture of Indian spices, more fragrant and slightly sweeter than curry powder. Does not contain turmeric that gives yellow color.

Garlic.

Allium sativum.
Origin: Northern Hemisphere
Parts: Bulb
Flavor: Strong, unique
Form: Whole, chips, powdered, juice
Uses: Culinary
Home garden: Outdoors

Germander.

Teucrium chamaedrys.
Origin: Europe, Southeast Asia
Parts: Leaves
Flavor: Mild
Form: Cut
Uses: Tea
Home garden: Outdoors

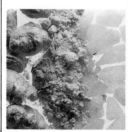

Ginger.

Zingiber officinale.
Origin: Southeast Asia
Parts: Rhizomes
Flavor: Strong, unique
Form: Whole, cut, ground, crystalized
Uses: Culinary
Home garden: Indoors/outdoors

Ginseng.

Panax species.
Origin: North America, Eastern Asia
Parts: Roots, leaves
Flavor: Strong, bitter
Form: Whole or powdered roots, cut leaves
Uses: Tea
Home garden: Outdoors

Goldenrod.

Blue Mountain tea.
Solidago odora.
Origin: United States
Parts: Flowering tops, leaves
Flavor: Mild
Form: Cut
Uses: Dye, tea, decoration
Home garden: Outdoors

Goldenseal.

Hydrastis canadensis.
Origin: United States
Parts: Roots
Form: Cut, powdered
Uses: Cosmetics
Home garden: Not recommended

Great mullein.

Aaron's rod.
Verbascum thapsus.
Origin: Europe, Asia
Parts: Leaves, flowers
Flavor: Mild
Form: Cut
Uses: Dye, fragrance, tea
Homegrown: Outdoors

Henna.

Lawsonia inermis.
Origin: North Africa,
Asia, Australia
Parts: Leaves
Form: Cut or ground
Uses: Dye, cosmetics
Home garden: Outdoors
as ornamental in warm
regions

Hibiscus.

Hibiscus rosa-sinensis.
Origin: Tropical Asia
Parts: Flowers
Form: Whole
Uses: Tea, dye
Home garden: Indoors/
outdoors in warm
regions, greenhouse

Hops.

Humulus lupulus.
Origin: Northern
temperate regions
Parts: Female flowers
Flavor: Bitter
Form: Whole
Uses: Beer
Home garden: Outdoors

Horehound.

Marrubium vulgare.
Origin: Asia, Europe,
North Africa, Azores,
Canary Islands
Parts: Leaves
Flavor: Bitter
Form: Cut
Uses: Tea, candy
Home garden: Outdoors

Horseradish.

Armoracia rusticana.
Origin: Southeast Europe
Parts: Fleshy roots
Flavor: Hot, pungent
Form: Powdered
Uses: Culinary
Home garden: Outdoors

Hyssop.

Hyssopus officinalis.
Origin: Europe
Parts: Leaves, flowers
Form: Cut
Uses: Fragrance,
decoration
Home garden: Outdoors

Indigo.

False indigo, wild indigo,
horsefly.
Baptisia tinctoria.
Origin: United States
Parts: Leaves, pods,
bark
Form: Cut
Uses: Dye
Home garden: Outdoors

Jasmine.

Jasminum species.
Origin: Asia, Africa,
Australia
Parts: Flowers
Scent: Sweet
Form: Petals
Uses: Tea, fragrance
Home garden: Indoors/
outdoors in warm regions

Juniper.

Juniperus communis.
Origin: North America,
Eurasia
Parts: Berrylike cones
Flavor: Slightly bitter
Form: Whole
Uses: Culinary, gin
flavoring, dye
Home garden: Outdoors

Kava-Kava.

Piper methysticum.
Origin: Pacific Islands
Parts: Roots
Flavor: Bitter
Form: Ground
Uses: Beverage
Home garden: Not
recommended

Kelp.

Seaweed.
Macrosytica pyrifera
(Atlantic) and *Fucus
versiculosus* (Pacific).
Origin: Oceans
Parts: Foliage
Flavor: Mild to bitter
Form: Cut
Uses: Culinary
Home garden: Not
recommended

Lady's Mantle.

Alchemilla vulgaris.
Origin: Europe
Parts: Leaves
Form: Cut
Uses: Fragrance,
decoration, dye
Home garden: Indoors/
outdoors

Lavender.

Lavandula species.
Origin: Europe
Parts: Leaves, blossoms
Form: Whole, cut
Uses: Fragrance,
decoration
Home garden: Indoors/
outdoors

Lemon balm.

Melissa officinalis.
Origin: Southern France
Parts: Leaves
Flavor: Lemonlike
Form: Crushed
Uses: Culinary, tea,
cosmetics, fragrance
Home garden: Indoors,
outdoors except in very
hot regions.

Lemongrass.

Oil grass, West Indian
lemongrass, fever grass.
Cymbopogon citratus.
Origin: India, Ceylon
Parts: Leaves, stems
Flavor: Lemonlike
Form: Cut
Uses: Tea, fragrance
Home garden: Not
recommended

Lemon verbena.

Aloysia triphylla.
Origin: Argentina, Chile
Parts: Leaves
Flavor: Lemonlike
Form: Cut
Uses: Culinary, fragrance, tea
Home garden: Indoors, greenhouse or outdoors in very mild climates.

Licorice.

Glycyrrhiza glabra.
Origin: Mediterranean, Asia
Parts: Roots
Flavor: Distinctive
Form: Sticks, pieces, powdered
Uses: Culinary, fragrance
Home garden: Outdoors

Lily-of-the-valley.

Convallaria majalis.
Origin: Europe
Parts: Leaves, flowers
Form: Cut
Uses: Dye (leaves), fragrance (flowers)
Home garden: Outdoors, greenhouse

Linden.

Tillia x europea.
Origin: Northern temperate zones.
Parts: Flowers, leaves
Flavor: Mild
Form: Whole
Uses: Cosmetics, tea
Home garden: Outdoors

Lotus.

Nelumbo species.
Origin: Asia, North America
Parts: Roots
Flavor: Subtle
Form: Sliced
Uses: Culinary
Home garden: Water gardens

Lovage.

Levisticum officinale.
Origin: Southern Europe
Parts: Seeds, stalks, leaves
Flavor: Celerylike
Form: Cut leaves and bark, whole seed
Uses: Culinary, decoration
Home garden: Outdoors, difficult along warm coasts

Mace.

Myristica fragrans.
Origin: Moluccas (Indonesia)
Parts: Seed coverings only (aril)
Flavor: Strong nutmeg
Form: Blades, ground
Uses: Culinary, fragrance
Home garden: Only in hot moist climates

Madder.

Rubia tinctorum.
Origin: Southern Europe, Asia Minor
Parts: Roots
Form: Cut
Uses: Dye
Home garden: Outdoors

Malva.

Malva sylvestris.
Origin: Europe
Parts: Flowers, leaves
Flavor: Delicate
Form: Cut leaves, whole flowers
Uses: Tea, decoration
Home garden: Outdoors

Marjoram.

Sweet marjoram.
Origanum majorana.
Origin: North Africa, southwest Asia
Parts: Leaves
Flavor: Mild, sweet
Form: Cut
Uses: Culinary
Home garden: Indoors/outdoors

Marsh mallow.

Althaea officinalis.
Origin: Europe
Parts: Roots, flowers, leaves
Flavor: Mild
Form: Cut leaves and roots, whole flowers
Uses: Tea, decoration
Home garden: Outdoors

Mint.

Mentha species.
Origin: Europe
Parts: Leaves
Flavor: Distinct, sweet
Form: Cut
Uses: Culinary, fragrance, tea, cosmetics
Home garden: Indoors/outdoors

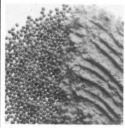

Mustard.

Brassica species.
Origin: Europe, Asia
Parts: Seeds
Flavor: Pungent
Form: Whole, powdered
Uses: Culinary
Home garden: Outdoors, mainly for fresh leaves, weedy

Myrrh.

Commiphora myrrha.
Origin: North Africa
Parts: Resin
Scent: Sweet, spicy
Form: Gum, powder
Uses: Fragrance
Home garden: Not recommended

Myrtle.

Myrtus communis.
Origin: Mediterranean
Parts: Leaves
Scent: Spicy
Form: Cut
Uses: Fragrance
Home garden: Outdoors

Nettle.
Urtica species.
Origin: Europe
Parts: Leaves
Uses: Dye, tea
Home garden: Not recommended

Nutmeg.
Myristica fragrans.
Origin: Moluccas (Indonesia)
Parts: Peeled seeds
Flavor: Spicy
Form: Whole, ground
Uses: Culinary, fragrance
Home garden: Only in hot moist climates

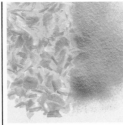

Oat straw.
Avena sativa.
Origin: Mediterranean
Parts: Stems
Flavor: Mild
Form: Cut
Uses: Tea
Home garden: Not recommended

Onion.
Allium cepa.
Origin: Northern Hemisphere
Parts: Bulbs
Flavor: Distinct, sweet to strong
Form: Whole, chopped, powdered
Uses: Culinary, dye (skin)
Home garden: Outdoors

Oregano.
Wild marjoram, pot marjoram.
Origanum vulgare.
Origin: Europe, Central Asia
Parts: Leaves
Flavor: Pungent
Form: Cut, powdered
Uses: Culinary, dye
Home garden: Indoors/outdoors

Orris.
Florentine iris, German iris.
Iris x germanica florentina.
Origin: Probably Mediterranean
Parts: Roots
Scent: Sweet
Form: Pieces, powdered
Uses: Fragrance, cosmetics
Home garden: Outdoors

Papaya.
Carica papaya.
Origin: Tropical America
Parts: Leaves
Form: Cut
Uses: Soap, cosmetics
Home garden: Outdoors in tropics only

Paprika.
Capsicum annuum Longum Group.
Origin: North and South America
Parts: Fruit pods
Flavor: Sweet, spicy
Form: Ground
Uses: Culinary
Home garden: Outdoors

Parsley.
Petroselinum crispum.
Origin: Europe, Western Asia
Parts: Leaves
Flavor: Mild
Form: Chopped
Uses: Culinary
Home garden: Indoors/outdoors

Passionflower.
Passiflora incarnata.
Origin: United States
Parts: Leaves, flowers
Flavor: Mild
Form: Cut
Uses: Tea
Home garden: Outdoors

Patchouli.
Pogosiemon patchouli.
Origin: India, Philippines
Parts: Leaves
Scent: Spicy, strong
Form: Cut, ground, powdered
Uses: Fragrance
Home garden: Not recommended

Pennyroyal.
Mentha pulegium.
Origin: Europe, Western Asia
Parts: Leaves
Flavor: Bitter
Form: Cut
Uses: Cosmetics, tea
Home garden: Indoors, outdoors in mild climates

Pepper.
Black pepper (with husk), white pepper (husk removed).
Piper nigrum.
Origin: India, Ceylon
Parts: Buds
Flavor: Distinct, hot
Form: Whole, cracked, ground
Uses: Culinary
Home garden: Not recommended

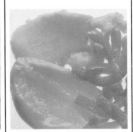

Pimento.
Capsicum annuum Grossum Group.
Origin: North and South America
Parts: Fruits
Flavor: Sweet, mild
Form: Whole, chopped
Uses: Culinary
Home garden: Outdoors

Plantain.
Plantago major.
Origin: Europe, Asia
Parts: Leaves
Form: Cut
Uses: Skin care
Home garden: Not recommended

Pomegranate.

Punica granatum.

Origin: Europe and South Asia
Parts: Bark, seeds
Flavor: Tart
Form: Cut bark, whole seed
Uses: Dye, culinary (seed)
Home garden: Outdoors in subtropical climates, greenhouse

Poppy.

Papaver somniferum.

Origin: Southeast Europe, Western Asia
Parts: Seeds
Flavor: Subtle
Form: Whole
Uses: Culinary
Home garden: Illegal in U.S

Red clover.

Trifolium pratense.

Origin: Europe
Parts: Flowers
Flavor: Subtle
Form: Whole, cut
Uses: Tea
Home garden: Not recommended

Redroot.

New Jersey tea, mountain sweet.

Ceanothus americanus.

Origin: United States
Parts: Roots
Flavor: Subtle
Form: Cut
Uses: Tea, dye
Home garden: Not recommended

Rose.

Rosa species.

Origin: Northern Hemisphere
Parts: Flowers, hips
Flavor: Sweet
Form: Petals cut, hips whole or crushed
Uses: Culinary, tea, cosmetics, fragrance
Home garden: Outdoors

Rosemary.

Rosmarinus officinalis.

Origin: Mediterranean
Parts: Leaves, flowers
Flavor: Spicy
Form: Whole, cut, ground
Uses: Culinary, tea, cosmetics, fragrance
Home garden: Indoors/outdoors

Safflower.

American saffron, false saffron.

Carthamus tinctorius.

Origin: Probably Eurasia
Parts: Flowers
Form: Cut
Uses: Culinary, dye, cosmetics, decoration
Home garden: Outdoors, best in dry climates

Saffron.

Crocus sativus.

Origin: Mediterranean
Parts: Flower stigmas
Flavor: Spicy
Form: Whole strands, ground
Uses: Culinary, dye
Home garden: Outdoors

Sage.

Salvia species.

Origin: Worldwide
Parts: Leaves
Flavor: Strong
Form: Cut, ground
Uses: Culinary, tea, fragrance, dye, decoration
Home garden: Indoors/outdoors

Sandalwood.

Santalum album.

Origin: India
Parts: Wood
Form: Chips, powdered
Uses: Fragrance
Home garden: Not recommended

Sarsaparilla.

Smilax species.

Origin: Tropical America
Parts: Roots
Form: Cut, powdered
Uses: Culinary, fragrance
Home garden: Greenhouse

Sassafras.

Sassafras albidum.

Origin: United States
Parts: Bark
Flavor: Rootbeer-like
Form: Cut
Uses: Culinary, fragrance, tea
Home garden: Outdoors

Savory.

Satureja species.

Origin: Mediterranean
Parts: Leaves
Flavor: Tangy (winter), sweet (summer)
Form: Cut
Uses: Culinary
Home garden: Indoors/outdoors

Sesame.

Benne.

Sesamum indicum.

Origin: Tropics
Parts: Seeds
Flavor: Nutty
Form: Whole
Uses: Culinary
Home garden: Outdoors in warm climates

Shallot.

Allium cepa Aggregatum Group.

Origin: Northern Hemisphere
Parts: Bulbs
Flavor: Delicate onionlike
Form: Whole, diced
Uses: Culinary
Home garden: Outdoors

Soapwort.

Saponaria officinalis.

Origin: Europe, Asia
Parts: Roots
Form: Cut
Uses: Soap substitute, cosmetics
Home garden: Not recommended

Southernwood.

Old-man.
Artemisia abrotanum.
Origin: Southern Europe
Parts: Leaves
Scent: Strong
Form: Cut
Uses: Fragrance, decoration
Home garden: Outdoors

Speedwell.

St. Paul's betony, gypsyweed.
Veronica officinalis.
Origin: Europe, Asia, North America
Parts: Leaves
Form: Cut
Uses: Tea
Home garden: Outdoors

St. John's Wort.

Hypericum species.
Origin: Temperate zones
Parts: Tops
Form: Cut
Uses: Cosmetics, dye
Home garden: Outdoors

Star anise.

Illicum verum.
Origin: China, Vietnam
Parts: Unripe fruits
Flavor: Spicy
Form: Whole
Uses: Culinary
Home garden: Outdoors in warm climates

Strawberry.

Woodland strawberry.
Fragaria vesca.
Origin: Eurasia, North America
Parts: Leaves
Flavor: Mild
Form: Cut
Uses: Tea
Home garden: Outdoors

Sumac.

Rhus glabra.
Origin: North America
Parts: Berries, roots, leaves
Form: Whole berries, cut roots and leaves
Uses: Dye
Home garden: Outdoors

Sunflower.

Helianthus annuus.
Origin: North America
Parts: Seeds
Flavor: Nutty
Form: Whole
Uses: Culinary
Home garden: Outdoors

Sweet flag.

Calamus.
Acorus calamus.
Origin: Northern Hemisphere
Parts: Roots
Scent: Sweet
Form: Cut, powdered
Uses: Fragrance
Home garden: Outdoors water garden

Tabasco.

Capsicum frutescens.
Origin: Tropical America
Parts: Fruits
Flavor: Hot
Form: Liquid sauce
Uses: Culinary
Home garden: Not recommended

Tansy.

Tanacetum vulgare.
Origin: Europe, Asia
Parts: Leaves, flowers
Form: Cut
Uses: Cosmetics, dye, decoration
Home garden: Outdoors

Tarragon.

Estragon.
Artemisia dracunculus.
Origin: Southern Europe, Asia, Western United States
Parts: Leaves
Flavor: Sweet
Form: Cut
Uses: Culinary
Home garden: Indoors/ outdoors

Tea.

Black, green or Oolong tea.
Camellia sinensis.
Origin: Asia
Parts: Leaves
Flavor: Distinct, aromatic
Form: Cut
Uses: Tea
Home garden: Outdoors as ornamental

Thyme.

Thymus species.
Origin: Europe, Asia
Parts: Leaves
Flavor: Slightly pungent
Form: Cut
Uses: Culinary, tea, fragrance
Home garden: Indoors/ outdoors

Turmeric.

Curcuma domestica.
Origin: Tropical Asia
Parts: Tuberous rhizomes
Flavor: Subtle
Form: Powdered
Uses: Culinary, dye
Home garden: Outdoors in warm climates, greenhouse

Valerian.

Allheal, garden helio-
trope, phew plant.
Valeriana officinalis.
Origin: Europe, Western
Asia
Parts: Roots
Form: Cut, powdered
Uses: Cosmetics
Home garden: Outdoors

Vanilla.

Vanilla planifolia.
Origin: Tropical America
Parts: Seed pods
Flavor: Unique, aromatic
Form: Fermented, whole,
powdered, liquid extract
Uses: Culinary, fragrance
Home garden: Green-
house as ornamental

Vervain.

Verbena species.
Origin: Tropical America
Parts: Leaves, roots
Flavor: Strong
Form: Cut
Uses: Tea
Home garden: Outdoors

Violet.

Viola odorata.
Origin: Europe, Africa,
Asia
Parts: Flowers, leaves
Fragrance: Sweet
Form: Cut leaves, whole
or candied flowers
Uses: Culinary, tea,
fragrance, cosmetics,
decoration
Home garden: Outdoors

Water chestnut.

Eleocharis dulcis.
Origin: Tropical Asia,
Pacific Islands, Mada-
gascar, West Africa
Parts: Tubers or corms
Flavor: Subtle
Form: Whole
Uses: Culinary
Home garden: Outdoor
water garden

Watercress.

Nasturtium officinale.
Origin: Europe
Parts: Leaves and stems
Flavor: Slightly peppery
Form: Cut
Uses: Culinary
Home garden: Outdoor
water garden

Wasabi.

Japanese horseradish.
Wasabi japonica.
Origin: Asia
Parts: Roots
Flavor: Very hot, pungent
Form: Powdered
Uses: Culinary
Home garden: Not
recommended

Wintergreen.

Teaberry, checkerberry,
mountain tea.
Gaultheria procumbens.
Origin: United States
Parts: Leaves
Flavor: Minty
Form: Cut
Uses: Culinary, tea,
cosmetics, fragrance
Home garden: Not
recommended

Witch hazel.

Hamamelis virginiana.
Origin: Eastern North
America
Parts: Leaves, bark
Form: Cut
Uses: Cosmetics
Home garden: Outdoors

Wood betony.

Bishop's wort,
woundwort.
Stachys officinalis.
Origin: Europe, Asia
Parts: Leaves, flowers
Scent: Strong, minty
Form: Cut
Uses: Tea, decoration
Home garden: Outdoors

Woodruff.

Sweet woodruff.
Galium odoratum.
Origin: Europe, North
Africa, Asia
Scent: Sweet
Form: Cut
Uses: Culinary, tea,
fragrance
Home garden: Indoors/
outdoors

Wormwood.

Artemisia absinthium.
Origin: Europe
Parts: Leaves
Fragrance: Strong, spicy
Form: Cut
Uses: Fragrance, insect
repellent, decoration
Home garden: Outdoors

Yarrow.

Achillea millefolium.
Origin: Europe, Western
Asia
Parts: Leaves, flowers
Scent: Strong
Form: Cut
Uses: Cosmetics, dye,
decoration
Home garden: Outdoors

Yellow dock.

Rumex crispus.
Origin: Europe, North
and South America
Parts: Roots (flowers
dried for decoration)
Form: Cut
Uses: Dye
Home garden: Not
recommended

Yerba-de-mate.

Mate, Paraguay tea.
Ilex paraguariensis.
Origin: South America
Parts: Leaves
Flavor: Strong
Form: Cut
Uses: Tea
Home garden: Not
recommended

Sources

We have room here to list only a few suppliers of herbs and spices. You may find others nearer you in *Herb Buyers' Guide* available for 50 cents from the Herb Society of America, 2 Independence Court, Concord, MA 01742.

Mail-order plants and seeds

In addition to the herb specialists listed below, most of the major vegetable and flower seed companies offer the common herbs in their garden catalogs. There may be a charge for the catalogs.

ABC Herb Nursery
Rt. 1, Box 313
Lecoma, MO 65540

Applewood Seed Co.
5380 Vivian St.
Arvada, CO 80002

Carpilands Herb Farm
Silver St.
Coventry, CT 06238

Carroll Gardens
Box 310
Westminster, Md 21157

Casa Yerba
Star Rt. 2, Box 21
Days Creek, OR 97429

Catnip Acres Farm
67 Christian St.
Oxford, CT 06483

Companion Plants
Rt. 6, Box 88
Athens, OH 45701

Country Herbs
Box 357
Stockbridge, MA 01262

Cricket Hill Herb Farm
RFD Box 420
Brookfield, NH 03872
(Preserved herbs also)

Earthstar Herb Gardens
438 W. Perkinsville Rd.
Chino Valley, AZ 86323
(Preserved herbs also)

Earthworks Herb Garden Nursery
923 N. Ivy St.
Arlington, VA 22201

Flintridge Herb Farm
Rt. 1, Box 187
Sister Bay, WI 54234

Fox Hill Farm
444 W. Michigan Ave.
Box 7
Parma, MI 49269

Halcyon Gardens Herbs
Box 124
Gibsonia, PA 15044

Hartman's Herb Farm
Old Dana Rd.
Barre, MA 01005
(Preserved herbs also)

Hemlock Hill Herb Farm
Litchfield, CT 06759

Herbs 'N Honey Nursery
16085 Airlie Rd.
Box 124
Monmouth, OR 97361

Hickory Hollow
Rt. 1, Box 52
Peterstown, WV 24963

Logee's Greenhouses
55 North St.
Danielson, CT 06239

Meadowbrook Herbs & Things, Inc.
Whispering Pines Rd.
Wyoming, RI 02898

Merry Gardens
Camden, ME 04843

The Naturalists
Box 435
Yorktown Heights, NY 10598

Nichol's Garden Nursery
1190 N. Pacific Hwy.
Albany, OR 97321
(Preserved herbs also)

Orenmoore Herbs
9708—208th Ave. East
Sumner, WA 98390

Otto Richter and Sons, Ltd.
Goodwood, Ontario, LOC 1A0
Canada
(Preserved herbs also)

Clyde Robin Seed Co.
Box 2366
Castro Valley, CA 94546

Roses of Yesterday and Today
802 Brown's Valley Rd.
Watsonville, CA 95076

Rutland of Kentucky
3 Bon Haven
Maysville, KY 41056

Sandy Mush Herb Nursery
Rt. 2, Surrett Cove Rd.
R2-OG
Leicester, NC 28748

Shady Hill Gardens
823 Walnut
Batavia, IL 60510

Sunny Border Nurseries, Inc.
1708 Kensington Rd.
Kensington, CT 06037

Sunnybrook Farms
Box 6
Chesterland, OH 44026

Tansy Farms
Dept. PH, PR1 Agassiz
British Columbia, VOM 1A0
Canada

Taylor's Herb Gardens, Inc.
1535 Lone Oak Rd.
Vista, CA 92083

Victoria Herb Gardens
Box 947
Southampton, PA 19866

Well-Sweep Herb Farm
317 Mt. Bethel Rd.
Port Murray, NJ 07865

Yankee Peddler Herb Farm
Hwy. 36 North
Brenham, TX 77833

Preserved herbs and spices

Many of these suppliers require rather large minimum orders. Write for price lists and offerings: their stocks change from time to time according to availability.

Fmali Herb Co.
831 Almar Ave.
Santa Cruz, CA 95060

Nature's Herb Co.
281 Ellis St.
San Francisco, CA 94102

Northwestern Coffee Mills
217 North Broadway
Milwaukee, WI 53202

Response Marketing
2861 La Cresta Ave.
Anaheim, CA 92806

San Francisco Herb Co.
250 14th St.
San Francisco, CA 94103

San Francisco Herb and Natural Food Co.
Box 40604
San Francisco, CA 94140

Tom Thumb Workshops-H
Box 332
Chincoteague, VA 23336

Wide World of Herbs
11 St. Catherine St. East
Montreal, Quebec, H2X 1K3
Canada

Whole Herb Co.
250 E. Blithedale Ave.
Mill Valley, CA 94941

Public Herb Gardens

In addition to the public places listed below, some commercial herb growers have display gardens at their home offices. Check our list of suppliers to see what may be located near you.

California
Arcadia:
The Herb Garden of the Los Angeles State and County Arboretum.

Sacramento:
Encina High School.

San Francisco:
Garden of Fragrance, Strybing Arboretum, Golden Gate Park.

Colorado
Denver:
The Molly Brown House and the Eugene Field House, Denver Botanic Garden.

Connecticut
Farmington:
Mary McCarthy Herb Garden, Farmington Museum.

Guilford:
Henry Whitfield House.

Delaware:
Odessa:
Corbit-Sharp House, Colonial Old Town.

District of Columbia
Washington:
Bishop's Garden, Washington Cathedral, Mount St. Albans.

National Herb Garden, United States National Arboretum.

Florida
Gainesville
Medicinal Plant Garden, University of Florida.

Georgia
Pine Mountain:
Callaway Gardens.

Illinois
Glencoe:
Botanic Garden, Chicago Horticultural Society.

Springfield
Lincoln's New Salem State Park.

Louisiana
St. Martinville:
The Acadian House Museum, Longfellow Evangeline State Park.

Maine
Rockport:
Vesper Chapel.

Maryland
Annapolis:
Slicer-Shiplap House.

Massachusetts
Pittsfield:
Hancock Shaker Village.

Plymouth:
Plimoth Plantation.

Sturbridge:
Old Sturbridge Village.

Michigan
Dearborn:
Greenfield Village.

Minnesota
Chaska:
Twin Cities Herb Society, University of Minnesota Landscape Arboretum.

Missouri
Lake Jacomo:
Missouri Town 1855, Jackson County Park.

Sainte Genevieve:
The Bolduc House.

St. Louis:
Missouri Botanical Gardens.

New Jersey
Gladstone:
Willowwood Arboretum.

Morristown:
Tempe Wick House, Jockey Hollow National Park.

Plainfield:
Cedar Brook Park.

Somerville:
The Duke Gardens.

Trenton:
William Trent House.

Woodbridge:
Bible Gardens, Beth Israel Memorial Park.

New York
Brooklyn:
Brooklyn Botanic Garden.

Ithaca:
Robinson York State Herb Garden, Cornell University.

New York City:
New York Botanical Garden, Bronx Park; Medieval Herb Garden, The Cloisters, Fort Tryon Park.

Old Westbury:
Old Westbury Gardens.

Rochester:
Garden of Fragrance, Rochester Museum and Science Center.

Southampton:
Thomas Halsey Homestead.

North Carolina
Manteo:
Elizabethan Garden, Roanoke Island.

Ohio
Cleveland:
Log House Herb Garden, Miles School Garden Center; Western Reserve Herb Society Garden, Garden Center of Greater Cleveland.

Oklahoma
Tulsa:
Anne Hathaway Municipal Herb Garden, Woodward Park.

Oregon
Portland:
Oregon Museum of Science and Industry.

Pennsylvania
Euphrata:
Beissel Kitchen Garden, Euphrata Cloister.

Harrisburg:
Ft. Hunter Mansion; William Penn Museum.

Kennett Square:
Longwood Gardens.

Lima:
Fragrant Garden, John J. Tyler Arboretum.

Morrisville:
Pennsbury Manor.

Philadelphia:
John Bartram's Garden, Drug Plant and Herb Garden, Morris Arboretum; Pennsylvania Hospital.

Pittsburg:
Old Economy Village; Pioneer Woman's Yarb Patch, Settler's Cabin Regional Park; Round Hill Regional Park; Winchester-Thurston School.

Rhode Island
Pawtucket:
Garden of Dye and Textile Plants, Old Slater Museum.

South Carolina
Charleston:
Charles Towne Landing; Heyward Washington House.

Roebuck:
Walnut Grove Plantation.

South Dakota
Brookings:
McCrory Gardens, South Dakota State University.

Utah
Salt Lake City:
University of Utah.

Virginia
Mt. Vernon:
Kitchen Garden.

Williamsburg:
John Blair Gardens; Wythe House.

Washington
Olympia:
Pioneer Herb Garden, Washington State Capitol Museum.

Wisconsin
Bayside
Schlitz Audubon Park.

Hales Corners:
Boerner Botanical Gardens, Whitnall Park.

Index

Boldface numbers indicate illustrations